TWAYNE'S WORLD AUTHORS SERIES
A Survey of the World's Literature

SPAIN

Janet Pérez, Texas Tech University

EDITOR

José Ortega y Gasset

TWAS 624

José Ortega y Gasset

JOSÉ ORTEGA Y GASSET

By VICTOR OUIMETTE
McGill University

TWAYNE PUBLISHERS
A DIVISION OF G.K. HALL & CO., BOSTON

Published in 1982 by Twayne Publishers,
A Division of G.K. Hall & Co.
All Rights Reserved

Printed on permanent/durable acid-free paper and bound
in the United States of America

First Printing

Library of Congress Cataloging in Publication Data

Ouimette, Victor.
  Jose Ortega y Gasset.

  (Twayne's world authors series. Spain ; TWAS 624)
  Bibliography: p. 164
  Includes index.
  1. Ortega y Gasset, José, 1883–1955
I Title.   II. Series.
B4568.074084   196'.1   81-6266
ISBN 0-8057-6466-6   AACR2

For María Elena, *luz vital*

Contents

About the Author

Preface

Chronology

1. The Life and Times of Ortega y Gasset   15

2. Rationalism, Objectivism, and Phenomenology   37

3. Perspectivism and Biologism   62

4. Ratiovitalism   86

5. Toward Historical Reason   112

6. The Practice of Historical Reason   127

7. Conclusion   150

Notes and References   155

Selected Bibliography   164

Index   171

About the Author

Victor Ouimette is associate professor of Spanish at McGill University in Montreal, Canada, where he has taught since 1968. He holds the B.A. from McGill University and the Ph.D. from Yale. He is the author of *Reason Aflame: Unamuno and the Heroic Will,* and he has contributed articles and reviews to various publications including *Hispania, Bulletin of Hispanic Studies, Revista Canadiense de Estudios Hispánicos.*

Preface

It is the purpose of this study to provide an orientation and a framework within which may be read and, it is hoped, savored, the works of one of the most fertile and influential minds of contemporary Spain. Frequently guilty of leaving his works unfinished, Ortega y Gasset, more than almost any other modern writer, demands a participation from the reader that will supplement his suggestions with the totality of his thought so that it may be possible to attempt to complete what he himself had promised to do. Therefore, it is my intention to suggest intellectual impulses throughout the half-century of his career which may contribute to a fuller understanding of any single work or problem. It is also my hope that many parallels and recurring concerns worthy of further study may at least be hinted at so that the reader will be able to establish his own web of connections for further study. Each reader must ultimately resolve the controversies surrounding every aspect of Ortega's work on the basis of his own reading of the texts.

This study is intended, then, not as an introduction to the philosophy of Ortega, something that has been well done by others, but rather as a sort of intellectual biography resting on the primary evidence of all of Ortega's available writings. Therefore, his political articles, which are far more important than has been recognized in most studies written before the publication of volumes 10 and 11 of his *Obras completas* [Complete Works], have been employed in order to show the close relationship between diverse facets of his intellectual, spiritual, and social activity.

The divisions that I have made in Ortega's career correspond to biographical, rather than purely philosophical, motives, and therefore do not always correspond to other, perfectly convincing, stages described by other critics. The translations into English, unless otherwise indicated, are all my own.

I would like to express my sincere gratitude to the Faculty of Graduate Studies and Research of McGill University for its generous financial assistance.

VICTOR OUIMETTE

McGill University

Chronology

1883   May 9: José Ortega y Gasset is born in Madrid.

1887   Ortega attends school in Córdoba.

1891–   Ortega attends the Jesuit school in Miraflores del Palo,
1897   Málaga.

1897–   Begins studies at the University of Deusto, Bilbao.
1898

1898   May: passes his first-year examinations in Salamanca before a
panel including Miguel de Unamuno.

1898–   Studies philosophy at the University of Madrid.
1904

1902   June: Ortega receives his *licenciatura* from the University of
Madrid. December: "Glosas," Ortega's first article, is published.

1904   December 15: Ortega receives his doctorate in Madrid.

1905   February: Ortega leaves for Germany via Paris. April–
November: studies at the University of Leipzig.

1906   June: awarded scholarship to continue studies in Germany.
Spends summer in Berlin and enrolls in University of Marburg in November.

1907   August: returns to Madrid.

1908   February: founds *Faro*, in Madrid. Enters into polemic with
Maeztu. June: appointed professor at the Escuela Superior
del Magisterio in Madrid. October: speaks at the Assembly for
the Progress of Science.

1909   Participates in many Socialist activities. Enters into polemic
with Unamuno.

1910   February: founds *Europa*. April 7: marries Rosa Spottorno
Topete. November: appointed Professor of Metaphysics at
University of Madrid.

1911   January to October: Ortega and wife in Marburg, with visits to
Florence and Bologna. May: birth of Miguel Germán in Marburg.

1912   Joins Republican Reform party.

1913   October: publishes Manifesto for the League for Political Education.

1914   March 23: founding meeting of the League for Political Education. July 21: publication of the *Meditaciones del Quijote* [Meditations on Quixote].

1915   Founds *España*.

1916   May: publication of first issue of *El Espectador*. July: Ortega and his father leave for Argentina. November: establishment of Committees of Defense, in Barcelona.

1917   January: Ortega returns to Madrid. June 11: "Bajo el arco en ruinas" provokes his separation from *El Imparcial*. December 1: *El Sol* appears.

1920   Urgoiti creates Calpe publishing house.

1921   *España invertebrada* [Invertebrate Spain] begins to appear in *El Sol*.

1922   December: articles of *El tema de nuestro tiempo* [The Modern Theme] begin to appear. "Biblioteca de Ideas del siglo XX" is founded under Ortega's direction. Death of Ortega Munilla.

1923   July: the first issue of *Revista de Occidente* appears. August: publication in book form of *El tema de nuestro tiempo*. September: General Primo de Rivera takes over the government.

1924   Book-publishing arm of *Revista de Occidente* is founded. January: first articles of *La deshumanización del arte* [The Dehumanization of Art] appear in *El Sol*. February: Unamuno is exiled by Primo de Rivera. December: first articles of *Ideas sobre la novela* [Ideas about the Novel] appear.

1926   July: Publication of first articles of *Estudios sobre el amor* [Studies on Love].

1927   March: publication begins of articles of *Mirabeau*. November: publication begins of "Ideas políticas," that would later become *La redención de las provincias*.

1928   March: Primo de Rivera forbids publication of one article of "Ideas políticas." August: Ortega leaves for second visit to Argentina. December: addresses Chilean Parliament.

1929   January: Ortega returns to Madrid. March: Primo de Rivera closes most Spanish universities; Ortega and others resign in protest. April–May: Ortega delivers public lectures on "What Is Philosophy?" October 24: first article of *La rebelión de las masas* [The Revolt of the Masses] appears in *El Sol*.

1930   January: Primo de Rivera resigns and leaves for Paris. February: Unamuno returns home from exile in France. November: Ortega openly criticizes the monarchy in *El Sol*.

1931   February: manifesto of the Group at the Service of the Republic. April 4: *Crisol* appears. April 12: Republican candidates win majority of urban seats in municipal elections. April 14: Alfonso XIII leaves Spain and the Second Republic is declared. June 28: Ortega is elected to the constituent Parliament. December 6: he calls for a "Rectification of the Republic."

1932   January 7: *Luz* appears. Spring: Parliament debates Catalonian autonomy. October: Ortega dissolves Group at the Service of the Republic.

1933   October: José Antonio Primo de Rivera founds the Falange Española.

1935   April: Ortega and Unamuno in Paris to attend opening of Spanish House at the University City. November 17: Ortega publishes his last article in a Spanish newspaper.

1936   March: Ortega receives Gold Medal of the City of Madrid. Spring: lecture tour in Holland. July 18: Civil War breaks out. August 30: Ortega leaves Madrid for France via Alicante. November: Ortega settles in Paris.

1937–   Winter in Paris.
1938

1938   Summer in Sant-Jean-de-Luz. October: Ortega undergoes gall-bladder surgery in Paris.

1939   February: Ortega moves to Portugal. April: Ortega's mother dies in Spain. August: Ortega leaves for Argentina.

1942   February: Ortega returns to settle in Estoril, Portugal.

1945   August: Ortega returns briefly to Spain.

1946   May 4: Ortega reads "The Idea of the Theater" at the reopening of the Madrid Ateneo.

1946,   Summers in San Sebastián.
1947

1948   Ortega acquires apartment at 28, Monte Esquinza, Madrid; with Julián Marías, founds the Instituto de Humanidades, which he inaugurates with *An Interpretation of Universal History.*

1949   July: attends Goethe bicentennial celebrations in Aspen, Colorado. September: lectures in Berlin, Hamburg, Munich, and Darmstadt.

1950   Instituto de Humanidades closed.

1951   Visits Marburg, Darmstadt, and Geneva; awarded honorary doctorate by University of Glasgow.

1953   Visits Germany.

1954 Visits Germany. October: visits England, speaks in Torquay.
1955 May: gives his last public lecture, in Venice. October 18: Ortega dies at home in Madrid, at 11:20 A.M.
1957 Publication of *El hombre y la gente* [Man and People], and *¿Qué es filosofía?* [What is Philosophy?]
1958 Publication of *La idea de principio en Leibniz* [The Idea of Principle in Leibniz], *Idea del teatro* [The Idea of the Theater], and *Goya*.
1959 Publication of *Velázquez*.
1960 Publication of *Una interpretación de la historia universal* [An Interpretation of Universal History] and *Meditación de Europa* [Meditation on Europe].
1963 April: *Revista de Occidente* is permitted to recommence monthly publication.
1966 Publication of *Unas lecciones de metafísica* [Some Lessons on Metaphysics].
1979 Publication of *Sobre la razón histórica*.

CHAPTER 1

The Life and Times of Ortega y Gasset

I The Political and Intellectual Background

Virtually the entire social and intellectual drama of Ortega's Spain was played out against the background of a confused and often hypocritical nineteenth century. A certain bizarre unity had been given to the second half of that century by the endless conflicts between a traditional and even fanatical Spain on the one hand and a liberal and often immoderate Spain on the other. The country had known no period of normalcy since the end of the seventeenth century, and the revolution and subsequent abdication of Queen Isabel II in 1868 represented a sort of turning point as the nation at large finally tired of the monarchy's ineptitude and the corruption that it had engendered. Five years later, a republic was established, with the hope that it would lead the nation into a sound future, but it too collapsed after little more than a year. Conflicts over the succession to the throne continued until December 1874, when the Bourbon monarchy was restored in the person of Alfonso XII. A false appearance of stability was imposed upon the country in a system of political gerrymandering created by the Conservative prime minister, Antonio Cánovas de Castillo, with the consent of the Liberal leader, Práxedes Sagasta, who agreed that the two parties would alternate in power. While this had the advantage of giving a sepulchral tranquility to Spanish politics, it also fomented disenchantment with the entire political process. As a result, the chasm between the people and the government became all but unbridgeable, and there was little popular participation in the system, especially in rural areas. Widespread abstention from voting made it easy and perhaps even necessary for a system of "bossism" (*caciquismo*) to take over and place effective power in the hands of the most influential people in each district. However effective it may have been, the process was merely a simulacrum of what it claimed to be, and was symbolic of national attitudes.

In her colonies, Spain was no less haunted by conflicts and uprisings, which culminated in 1898 when the United States declared war
on a Spain that was militarily, politically, and psychologically unprepared. Spain had lost the war before the first shot was fired and was
obliged to sign a treaty that stripped her of virtually all her overseas
possessions. The financial losses were enormous and the economy
was dangerously weakened for years, yet a mood of cynicism, indifference, and lethargy continued to permeate the country. In the
years preceding the debacle, three men in particular had devoted
themselves to trying to bring about a renewed alertness in the
Spanish intellect. They were Julián Sanz del Río (1814–1869); his
follower, Francisco Giner de los Ríos (1839–1915); and Joaquín Costa
(1844–1911). Sanz del Río had imported into Spain a sort of idealism
that had its roots in the thought of Karl Christian Friedrich Krause
(1781–1832), a professor at the University of Heidelberg and a
younger contemporary of Kant. From 1857 until his death, Sanz
propagated his very personal interpretation of Krausism, which represented an ingenious adaptation to the arid intellectual soil of the
Peninsula of a mode of thought and a code of conduct that greatly
appealed to the more liberal sectors of the evolving Spanish middle
class, and corresponded to their belief in and desire for progress.

Krausism aspired, rather vaguely, to ideals of universal fraternity
and "harmonic rationalism," but its real importance lay in what it was
as a way of life and what it achieved for decades of Spanish life through
its philosophy of education. Because of its conviction that man must
be prepared to enter upon the new stage of spiritual development
that it believed was at hand, Krausism lay great store by science and
technology. Moreover, stripped of its metaphysics, it did suggest a
path toward social and spiritual renewal. Despite the violent attacks
launched by the traditionalists, the Krausist philosophy began to be
widely applied to the entire system of Spanish education in the
liberalizing euphoria that followed the Revolution of September
1868. In 1869 a significant move was made toward incorporating
women into the intellectual and social life of the country when the
Escuela de Institutrices (Women's Normal School) was opened, but
the most important organism opened its doors in October 1876: the
Institución Libre de Enseñanza ("Institution of Free Instruction"), a
sort of private school for some two hundred boys, with one of the
finest teaching staffs that could be recruited, and under the direction
of Giner. Giner's thought stressed education, not just of the intellect,
but of the total being, and this meant a system of direct learning by

means of excursions, physical exercise, and manual labor.[1] Since it was necessary to start with the youngest members of society so that the reform would eventually reach all levels, a primary school was opened in 1878.

The other great presence in the social thought of the time was Joaquín Costa, a simple man from the northeastern interior who taught Spanish History and Administrative Law in the Institution. He was, above all, a philosopher of law who believed that the central state must relinquish certain powers for the benefit of other organisms that were closer to the daily life of the people, and particularly of the individual, to whom he gave special importance in the social structure. Like Giner, he believed that Krausism could reduce the role of the state and contribute to a harmonic system, free from doctrinairism and an exaggerated attention to form. In the years after the defeat of 1898, Costa was naturally converted into the leader of the "regenerationist" faction of the Spanish intelligentsia. His call for an "Iron Surgeon," capable of leading the country, provoked great enthusiasm among many of the younger members of the Generation of 1898 and contributed in no small way to the fervor that they would show for Nietzsche and his Superman.[2]

II   *The Early Life of Ortega y Gasset*

José Ortega Munilla, father of the philosopher, was born of Spanish parents in 1856 in Cuba, where his father briefly held a judicial post. Two years later, the family returned to Spain, where the young José was educated. Despite his firm classical formation, his liberal attitudes were soon evident. At the age of nineteen, he embarked upon a career as a highly popular novelist and later became a journalist and a member of the administrative board of the Institución Libre de Enseñanza. He worked for various newspapers, founded a literary review, and in 1879, at the age of twenty-three, became editor of *Los Lunes,* the literary supplement of the finest and fairest newspaper in Madrid, *El Imparcial,* which had been founded in 1869 by Eduardo Gasset y Artime (1832–1884), also a director of the Institución Libre and a collaborator of Giner de los Ríos.[3]

The newspaper was a direct result of the liberal tendencies emanating from the overthrow a year earlier of Isabel II. Distinguished for its impartiality and its modern methods of gathering news, it deservedly conquered a position of great authority in the last three decades of the century. Ortega Munilla was soon admitted to the family circle of the paper's founder, where he met and soon married María de los Dolores Gasset Chinchilla, the third of six children. Ortega Munilla continued to direct *Los Lunes* until 1906 and especially encouraged the work of younger writers, for whom publication there soon became a sign of considerable success.

After the death in 1884 of Eduardo Gasset, the newspaper was directed by his son, Rafael (1866–1927), until 1900 when his political ambitions carried him into the Conservative cabinet. His new career had a profound effect on the character of *El Imparcial,* which gradually became less true to both its traditions and its name as it tended to reflect too closely the politics of its owner. From 1900 until 1906, Ortega Munilla served as editor of the entire newspaper, and in 1902 he was received into the Royal Spanish Academy for his work as a novelist.

Shortly after their marriage, Ortega Munilla and his wife had moved to 4, Calle Alfonso XII, on the Plaza de la Independencia, and there on May 9, 1883, was born José, the second of their four children. His childhood was one of balance: baptized in the Royal Basilica of Atocha, he was brought up in the stimulating atmosphere of a house filled with his father's friends and associates, the leading politicians and writers of the country. There was an air of tolerance and liberalism fostered by his father, and of love, religion, and understanding generated by his mother.

José's first summers were spent in or near Madrid, but in 1887 the family began a tradition of vacationing in El Escorial, the site of the royal palace and monastery, built by Philip II some forty kilometers outside the capital. At first they occupied a house on the outskirts of town, but soon they rented an apartment within the royal complex itself. A great part of their family life would take place there over the next forty years, and its presence would be frequently sensed in José's work. It was in El Escorial that he first learned to read, under the tutelage of Manuel Martínez, who, according to his older brother Eduardo, "was the first to proclaim José's astonishing intellectual precociousness."[4] In fact, at the age of seven, José undertook successfully to memorize the entire first chapter of *Don Quixote,* in order to win a horse from his parents.

Summer vacations were also spent in Saint-Jean-de-Luz, in the French Pyrenees, and in Granada. Winters were occasionally spent in Córdoba, where Rafael Gasset had property, and frequent visits were made to Guadalajara as well, where he also owned land. The boys also benefited from visits to museums in the company of the art historian Francisco Alcántara. Because of their mother's health, the family moved in the winter of 1887–88 to their newly constructed house near Córdoba,[5] where Eduardo and José were enrolled in school under the direction of José del Río y Labandeira, a friend of their father. Among their classmates was Fernando de los Ríos, later to become professor of law at the University of Granada and an outstanding figure in the Socialist party.

From September 1891 until 1897, the two older boys were pupils at the Jesuit school of San Estanislao de Kostka in Miraflores del Palo, Málaga, where they studied under Father Gonzalo Colomer, brother of the well-known novelist Luis Colomer. Father Colomer recognized José's exceptional ability and gave him his first real taste of the classics. José received excellent marks and in every year but the last he led his class. His religious training was equally sound, and he entered the Marian Sodality in 1891, becoming prefect of the congregation in 1894 and 1895. The fact that the eldest sons of a distinguished liberal and skeptic, with strong ties to the Institución Libre, should be educated in a Jesuit school is not easily explained. Clearly, their mother's influence must be considered, although Eduardo attributed it rather to the outdated reputation of the Order for culture and to the absence of good public or private education in the Spain of that time.[6] In any case, he claimed, their father attempted to undo any harm by devoting the summers to opening their minds further. The experience with the Jesuits was decisive for both brothers, and upon finishing their studies, Eduardo reports that José was delighted to escape, saying, "If we had continued there, we would have ended up like the Indians in the missions of Paraguay: automata whose movements were governed by the bells that were rung by some of the 'reverends.'"[7] Several years later, José claimed that the only thing that the Jesuits did for him was to make him timid and pedantic.[8] His intellectual and imaginative development seems not to have been impeded, however, for it was during this period that, under the influence of his father, his extensive reading of Balzac excited him to such an extent that he was bedridden for days with a sort of nervous exhaustion, feeling that he had already lived several lives.[9] Alexandre Dumas and Jules Verne also served to stimulate his imagination, and his awareness of the recent Spanish past was awakened by the immensely popular *Episodios nacionales* of Benito Pérez Galdós.

The experience at Miraflores notwithstanding, in November 1897 José followed Father Colomer and enrolled in the Jesuit University of Deusto, in Bilbao, with the intention of studying philology and Greek under the well-known scholar Julio Cejador y Frauca. He remained at Deusto studying philosophy and some law until May 13, 1898, when he passed with a grade of "outstanding" his first-year examinations at the University of Salamanca before a panel that included the dean of the faculty, Miguel de Unamuno, whose intellectual peer he would soon become. It was also around this time that José began to write seriously, and his younger brother speaks of a short novel that he composed, presumably his only foray into fiction.[10]

From October 1898 until December 1904 he studied philosophy at the University of Madrid, where he became a close friend of Ramiro de Maeztu, with whom he shared an enthusiasm for Nietzsche and from whom he claimed to have received his interest in philosophy. In 1902 he published his first article, although not in the family newspaper, *El Imparcial,* where his first contribution dates from March 1904. He received his licentiate in June 1902 and his doctorate on December 15, 1904, with a thesis entitled *Los terrores del año mil* [The Terrors of the Year 1000], his first historical study, which was published in 1909. During 1903 he had begun his long correspondence with Unamuno, who gave him his first important public boost when he referred to him in an article in May 1904.[11]

III   Ortega in Germany

In late February 1905, following the pattern established by Sanz del Río, Ortega left for Germany. He traveled by train to Paris, which disappointed him, and then on to Cologne and finally Leipzig, where he remained at the university from April until November. Domingo Marrero speculates that he may have been attracted by the work in experimental psychology then being carried out by Wilhelm Wundt, with whom he may have taken a course.[12] He endured penury and, since he arrived with no knowledge of German, bitter loneliness that he attempted to alleviate by placing advertisements for conversation exchanges with other students. These months further opened him to both German and classical cultures, and he developed such enthusiasm for Latin and Greek that he temporarily set aside the study of philosophy and considered dedicating himself to philology and linguistics. He also studied ethics and attended courses in anatomy and histology. Through his random readings in the library, itself a great revelation, he began to refine his sense of the inadequacy of studies of Spanish history and civilization and the insufficiencies of Spanish educational values. It was here also that he first encountered

Kant's *Critique of Pure Reason,* which, with the experience of Leip-zig, convinced him of the need for the young to be given a strong ethical and ideological formation by their elders so that they might have a solid basis upon which to construct their own point of view.[13]

He was back in Madrid in the spring of 1906 and in June was awarded a scholarship by the state to continue his studies in Germany on the "prehistory of Philosophic Criticism." Although he later said that his grant was so small when converted into German marks that he could afford to eat only in the automats,[14] he was at least no longer financially dependent upon his father, whose relationship with his son was often cool to the point of hostility. This time, he went to Berlin, where, as he was later to regret, he did not meet the two outstanding figures of contemporary German philosophy who would later interest him greatly: Wilhelm Dilthey, who was by then profes-sor emeritus, and Georg Simmel.[15] Rather, he appears to have devoted himself to private studies as an auditor at the university. In November he enrolled in the University of Marburg, where he remained until August 1907. There, immersed in "the citadel of neo-Kantianism" (VIII, 32), he studied Kant and the history of modern philosophy with Hermann Cohen, and psychology and pedagogy with Paul Natorp, as well as attending seminars given by each of them. As he later recognized, from Cohen "I learned to extract the dramatic quality that really lies in every great problem; rather, that every problem of ideas is" (VIII, 34).

In many ways, Marburg overwhelmed Ortega, and he left with many concepts and attitudes that he would later modify and even reject. He was impressed by the fact that German scholars had a material ease that greatly facilitated their work, and realized that until the same was true in Spain, no serious scientific progress could originate in the Peninsula. He acquired a sense of the importance of a system for philosophical thought and a great respect for method. Neo-Kantianism also convinced him that ideas were of more impor-tance than individuals, an attitude that he was to hold for several years, and that replaced his youthful enthusiasm for Nietzsche. How-ever, he was soon to reject the neo-Kantian vision of how things *ought* to be, as opposed to how they are, and to consider it to have been a borrowed, inauthentic ideology in those who propounded it.[16] While in Marburg he formed many important personal contacts and the entire German experience convinced him of the importance of the rigorous application of modern scientific techniques to all aspects of social renewal.

IV   Ortega in Spain

In February 1908, he was back in Madrid, where he began to put his beliefs into practice by founding *Faro* [Beacon], a weekly magazine that was but the first of his many publishing ventures, and which he intended as a vehicle for the critical ideas of Spanish youth, his own generation. It was, however, dominated by members of the Generation of 1898. It was a journal of breadth, including regular sections devoted to social and political news and commentary, both foreign and domestic, as well as sections devoted to news of science and industry, economics, and foreign and Spanish books. The first issue appeared on February 2, 1908, and the last, number 54, appeared on February 28, 1909. It was a concrete sign that, in many ways, 1908 was the year Ortega's public career began. He sustained a polemic with the Conservative Gabriel Maura regarding the nature of liberalism, and another with Maeztu, who was then in London, regarding the relative superiority of men or ideas.

In June he was appointed professor of Psychology, Logic, and Ethics at the Escuela Superior del Magisterio (Normal School), which he had helped found, and in the last week of October, at the Assembly for the Progress of Science, held in Zaragoza, he spoke vigorously in favor of regenerating Spain by bringing her fully into the current of modern Europe. It was this belief that was to lead to his break with Unamuno in 1909. Harsh judgments had been emitted in Europe in the light of the severe government repression that had recently taken place in Barcelona, and Unamuno had defended certain Spanish values. Ortega responded with little grace, insulting Unamuno by name. It was, in any case, a highly charged moment for Spanish intellectuals in their search for a new ethical orientation, and the events of that period became a sort of watershed for them. Nonetheless, Ortega had clearly taken the decision that he must establish his own authority.

Upon his return from Germany, and simultaneous with his entrance into public life, Ortega's sympathies for socialism became manifest. In 1909 he participated in several Socialist meetings and on October 15 he made a strong speech attacking the government. As a result, he was invited to speak in the Casa del Pueblo ("People's House") in Madrid, where his enthusiasm for the integrity and discipline of socialism was given voice, as well as his reservations regarding Marxism and Socialist internationalism. For the next few years, the majority of his energies were devoted to political commentary. In

February 1910, he founded another magazine, *Europa*, which, as the title indicates, was a vehicle intended to contribute to the integration of Spain into the progressive life of the Continent, but like its predecessor, *Faro*, it lasted only a year.

On October 8, 1910, Ortega appeared before a jury established to select a successor to Nicolás Salmerón as professor of Metaphysics at the University of Madrid, and in early November he received the appointment, a signal distinction for a man of twenty-seven. The new post notwithstanding, Ortega's loyalty caused him to retain his position at the Escuela Superior del Magisterio, although he refused to accept his salary there.

After a long engagement, Ortega had married on April 7, 1910, Rosa Spottorno y Topete in the bride's home in Madrid, and from January to October 1911, the couple spent a delayed honeymoon in Germany. Except for visits to Bologna and Florence, most of their time was spent in Marburg where Ortega visited Hermann Cohen, who was then writing his aesthetics. It was in Germany that Ortega's first child was born, in May 1911, and given the symbolic name of Miguel Germán. Upon his return to Spain, Ortega published in *El Imparcial*, on December 1, 1911, "The Case of Italy," regarding the war in Tripoli. The article, upon which *El Imparcial* itself was moved to comment, provoked a visit of protest by the Italian ambassador to Canalejas, the president of the cabinet. On December 14 Ortega defended himself in "More about the Case of Italy." Clearly, his political opinions were being heard at very high levels.

Ortega's first recorded entry into a political party took place in 1912, when he joined the Republican Reform party, recently founded by Gumersindo de Azcárate and Melquíades Alvarez, two important figures of the Institución Libre. The party preached tolerance, democracy, education, and the secularization of the state, and seemed to Ortega less dogmatic than the Socialist party, although their attitudes were very similar. One more indication of his growing prestige was evident in June 1913, when he served as secretary of the Congress of Sciences, held in Madrid. His association with *El Imparcial*, though, was beginning to show signs of strain as he intensified his attacks on the established political parties. In the fall of 1913 he devoted himself to the creation of a new national party, intended to go beyond the existing parties and unite a broader spectrum of Spaniards. Unamuno was invited to join in the effort but, not surprisingly, declined. Called the League for Political Education, it so occupied Ortega's time that from September 1913 until September

1914 his name virtually disappeared as an active journalist. He had
not abandoned his philosophical concerns, however, for at the same
time he began to write his first book, *Meditaciones del Quijote*
[Meditations on Quixote].

On March 23, 1914, in the Teatro de la Comedia in Madrid, Ortega
made his most important political speech to date, "Vieja y nueva
política" [Old and New Politics], the inaugural event of the League
for Political Education. Unfortunately, despite the extensive public-
ity, the speech was vague and ambiguous and went largely misun-
derstood. Nonetheless, the publication on July 21 of the *Meditations
on Quixote* converted Ortega into one of the most important intellectual figures in Spain. His only peer was Unamuno, whose *Del
sentimiento trágico de la vida* had been published a year before and
may well have had a role to play in the writing of Ortega's book.
Official sanction of his stature came on November 22, when he was
elected to the Royal Academy of Moral and Political Sciences. He
failed, however, to take formal possession of his seat.

V   *From* "España" *to the* "Revista de Occidente"

1915 opened with the publication of the highly influential *España*,
which Ortega directed for over a year, in a manner that reflected the
aims of the league. It had an exceptional role in the intellectual life of
the country, and included the collaboration of all the most important
members of the Generation of 1898. *España* had its editorial offices at
11, Calle del Prado, and it was there that Ortega, like his father at
home, first held his famous *tertulias,* which he dominated with the
charm and conversational brilliance for which he was always to be
famous. Many were to comment that Ortega spoke even better than
he wrote,[17] and although many outstanding figures attended, others,
like Unamuno, felt overshadowed at what they saw as a ceremony
dedicated to Ortega's own exaltation, and systematically avoided it
and him. In any case, *España* was for eight years the center for the
generation of writers who would later create the new Republic.
Ortega set the highest standards for the magazine: a handsomely
illustrated publication, it was carefully edited, varied, and attractively
readable. Within a year, however, his growing pessimism caused him
to leave this magazine also.

Ortega's next publishing venture was *El Espectador* [The
Spectator], of which the first issue appeared in May 1916. This was a
unique undertaking, for Ortega alone was responsible for writing all

of it, and it was sold by private subscriptions, which reached the astonishing total of 3,000. It contained both previously published articles and new ones, and although it showed a tendency to be moderately entertaining, many outstanding serious essays also appeared in it. A total of eight issues were published at very irregular intervals until 1934.

In July 1916 Ortega, his father, and other Spanish intellectuals left for Argentina, where, between August and October, Ortega gave a series of lectures at the University of Buenos Aires on Kant and the character of contemporary philosophy. Enormously successful, the lectures provoked invitations for him to speak also in Córdoba, Tucumán, Rosario, and Mendoza, and this success seems finally to have proven to his father that José was indeed the brilliant young man whom he had been reluctant to recognize.[18] Ortega's entire stay in Argentina was a revelation for him as he discovered a new world that fascinated him. What is more, it demonstrated dramatically that not only was Spain's relationship with Europe inadequately developed, but so too was her link with her former colonies where the future was being created and which were hungry for new ideas that Spain should have been able to provide. He found the visit flattering and rewarding, and left Buenos Aires on January 2, 1917, with some regret.

His isolation in Buenos Aires as well as his many other concerns kept him virtually removed from political commentary until June 11, 1917, when he published in *El Imparcial* his article "Bajo el arco en ruina" [Beneath the Arch in Ruins], in which he commented favorably on many of the aims of the Committees of Defense that had been formed by army officers in Catalonia, and that offered a direct threat to the political structure of Restoration Spain. The article precipitated his definitive separation from *El Imparcial*, coming as it did at a time of internal strife at the paper. Ortega joined a new daily paper then being founded with the extensive and enlightened financial backing of Nicolás María de Urgoiti, of La Papelera Española, a gigantic paper company that was looking for ways of selling its surplus production.[19] On December 1, 1917, *El Sol* [The Sun] appeared on the streets of Madrid.

El Sol was probably the finest newspaper Spain has ever seen. Ortega owned only a few shares of stock, but his was the ideological presence that shaped the paper. Between 1917 and 1931, it was not a profitable venture, but its influence was felt throughout the highest strata of the nation. Generously conceived, its aim was that suggested by its name: "above all, a desire to see things clearly" (X, 368; 1917). Moreover, the participation of outstanding thinkers gave it a unique authority in its attempts to expand the Spanish horizons. Its news was presented with a thoroughness and fairness hitherto unknown in Spain; its technical resources were of the most modern; its presentation and typography were appealing; and Ortega published about two-thirds of all his work there over the next years, including both signed articles and anonymous editorials. By 1920, *El Sol* had acquired such influence that a Royal Order required, in effect, that it price itself out of existence. Ortega fought vigorously against the measure, but the paper adapted and continued to publish. That same year, Urgoiti created a new publishing house, Calpe, that in 1922 would join with another to form one of the largest in Spain, Espasa-Calpe. One of its collections, the "Biblioteca de Ideas del Siglo XX" [Library of Twentieth-Century Ideas], established in 1922, was placed under the personal direction of Ortega, who promised, "In it I shall collect the works most characteristic of the new times, where thoughts that have not been thought before begin their lives" (VI, 305; 1922.)

In 1921 Ortega had again begun to reduce his journalistic activity in order to devote himself to more substantial works and to the preparation of the third issue of *El Espectador,* and the two editions of *España invertebrada* [Invertebrate Spain] that appeared that year. His father died in 1922, and in December Ortega began to publish in *El Sol* the essays that would appear in book form as *El tema de nuestro tiempo* [The Modern Theme] in 1923. It was a period of relative, but temporary, isolation from the hurly-burly of daily politics. His reputation was rapidly growing abroad and in January 1923 his first article to be published in a language other than Spanish appeared in the *Nouvelle Revue Française,* in Paris. The scope of his activities had also been greatly broadened by his close contacts with the Residencia de Estudiantes ("Students' Residence") which gave him the opportunity of meeting distinguished artists and intellectuals who were passing through Madrid. Many of these visitors attended his *tertulias* and helped keep him and his followers abreast of the times.

Ortega was clearly a force to be reckoned with in the 1920s, and one of his most significant accomplishments was the establishment of the *Revista de Occidente* [Review of the West], a monthly review that first appeared in July 1923 and lasted under his direction until the outbreak of the Civil War. Ortega financed the venture by raising money from his friends and he himself attended to every detail of the *Revista,* including the design for a unique new typeface, the ample margins, the high-quality paper, and, above all, the participation of the outstanding figures of the time, from throughout the West, as promised by the title. While many of the articles were translations of works previously published abroad, many were original contributions. The concerns of the *Revista* were not merely literary or political, but also embraced the latest developments of European science and philosophy. A great deal of attention was paid to new books and, after the formation in 1924 of a publishing house associated with the magazine, Ortega was able to form a team of outstanding translators whose work served both enterprises. The first issue of the *Revista de Occidente* was so successful that it was possible to publish the second issue in August, a month earlier than planned. Nonetheless, its press run of 3,000 copies rarely sold out. About half the copies went to South America, and the rest were distributed among the university and professional classes in Spain.[20]

In September 1923, the political situation that Ortega had so constantly criticized in the pages of *El Sol* made possible and perhaps even necessary the establishment of a Military Directory (dictatorship) under General Miguel Primo de Rivera. This came about by means of a theatrical coup that had the tacit support of the king and, although it was, on the whole, a benevolent dictatorship, its effect on intellectual life was deadly. Unamuno was sent into exile in February 1924 and eventually joined forces with Ortega's brother Eduardo, but Ortega, it must be said, flourished under the dictatorship, partly because of his own merits, partly because of the lack of serious competition for intellectual hegemony, and partly because his ideas and objectives were not unlike those that Primo de Rivera claimed to espouse. Primo greatly admired Ortega, whom he could not possibly understand, and the freedom with which Ortega functioned in those years, despite prior censorship, reveals not only his privileged position, but also his own caution in his writings. Moreover, he felt that the dictatorship had become inevitable, given the character and lack of political astuteness of his compatriots.

The *Revista de Occidente* became the principal organ of the intellectual elite and, along with Ortega's *tertulias* in the offices on the Avenue Pi y Margall, helped to foster the new poetical generation, the "Generation of 1927." Publication in the *Revista* and acceptance into the *tertulias* were signs of considerable intellectual success in the years of the Dictatorship,[21] and brought about a decisive change in the hierarchy of Spanish intellectuals. When the political changes began to exert new pressures on many of the *Revista*'s collaborators, a large number drifted away to devote themselves to political writings.

The magazine no longer fulfilled the same function in the intellectual life of the Republic, but throughout its life, the youthfulness of its contributors gave it an "air of perpetual vanguard."[22]

VI   *The Intellectual Leader*

During at least the first four years of the Dictatorship, Ortega's intellectual career was inhibited in no significant way. Undoubtedly he subjected himself to considerable self-censorship in his commentaries, and his works were generally better received by conservatives than by liberals because of his growing criticism of the masses and his interest in associating with high society.[23] He was one of the three or four most important figures of the day and his political stance remained ambiguous as he preferred to devote himself to questions of cultural anthropology and social behavior.

On January 1, 1924, the first article of *La deshumanización del arte* [The Dehumanization of Art] appeared in *El Sol,* and in April the book publishing house of the *Revista de Occidente* produced its first volume, a translation by Ortega of Lord Dunsany's *A Dreamer's Tales.* On December 12, *El Sol* began publication of the articles that would make up *Ideas sobre la novela* [Ideas about the Novel]. In February 1925 Ortega wrote a pair of articles, "On Fascism," in which his ambivalence was mixed with a more conservative tone than he had previously shown, and in July the fourth issue of *El Espectador* appeared, containing his controversial article "Conversation on the Golf Course or the Idea of 'Dharma,'" which offended many liberals because it showed an Ortega playing the part of oracle for Spanish high society, completely beyond the reach of political commitment. In July 1926 the articles of *Estudios sobre el amor* [Studies on Love] began to appear in *El Sol,* and in May 1927 the fifth volume of *El Espectador* was published, to be followed in July by *El espíritu de la letra* [The Spirit of the Letter], a collection of short pieces.

Ortega had begun a gradual return to political analysis at the end of 1925 with the publication of a series of articles evaluating the former Conservative prime minister, Antonio Maura, who had just died. In March 1927 he wrote *Mirabeau,* in which he made a splendid examination of the psychological nature of the great politician, and in November he began seriously to redirect his attention to the current Spanish situation in a series of "Political Ideas," articles devoted to his belief that the way out of the political and social impasse lay in the radical reorganization of Spain into large districts. This was an attempt to avoid the censorship that would certainly have affected his articles had he made it too evident that he was preaching a new form of regionalism. Such "camouflage" (Ortega's word) was finally of little avail as, in March 1928, the general himself forbade publication of one article that reached the inevitable conclusion that both economic and political autonomy were required for the regions.

In August 1928 Ortega left again for Buenos Aires at the invitation of the Society of Friends of the Arts. Throughout the fall he gave two series of lectures: one for his hosts, and another at the University, on "An Introduction to the Present" and "Hegel and Historiology."[24] Treated lavishly by his hosts, in November he crossed the Andes to Chile, where he gave four lectures to audiences of more than six thousand people, according to *El Sol*. He stayed at the Spanish embassy in Santiago and, in December, he addressed the Chilean Parliament. On January 5, 1929, he embarked in Montevideo for Lisbon, and returned to Madrid on January 20. The visit had been a great triumph and was given extensive coverage by the two newspapers that regularly published Ortega's work: *El Sol*, and *La Nación*, of Buenos Aires. Upon his arrival in Madrid he reaffirmed his belief that Argentina was the land of the future and, with considerable paternalism, commented on the charming quaintness of Chile.[25]

Life was not to be peaceful for Ortega after his return, for the dictatorship was crumbling and a series of measures that had begun in March 1928 giving university status to the religious universities of Deusto and El Escorial greatly offended many Spanish students, whose opposition broke into the open in March 1929, when they stoned the residence of Primo de Rivera. On March 16, the government closed the University of Madrid, but within three weeks the conflict had spread to nearly all the other universities, which the government also closed. Ortega and several other distinguished professors, including Fernando de los Ríos, resigned their chairs in protest and Ortega took his protest to the public by announcing that he would continue to give his interrupted course in the Cine Rex, in the Calle Mayor. Attendance was open to anyone willing to pay the relatively modest fee of thirty pesetas, or fifteen pesetas for people under the age of twenty-five. Despite the facts that the announced topic was "What is Philosophy?" and that the treatment would be "strictly philosophical,"[26] Ortega's appearance on stage on April 9 was greeted by a long ovation from an audience estimated at over four hundred. The lectures had been extensively advertised in *El Sol* and were fully reported as they took place on Tuesdays and Fridays at seven P.M. Their success caused the management of the theater to publish a request that the audience remain in the auditorium after each lecture and refrain from discussions in the lobby, where they obstructed access to the rest of the building. Ortega postponed the fifth lecture because of illness, and by the time of the sixth lecture it had become necessary to move the course to a larger theater, the Infanta Beatriz, in the Calle Claudio Coello. While many members of the audience were sincerely interested in what Ortega had to say, a large segment consisted of snobs and celebrity-seekers for whom the philosopher was a fashionable trophy.[27] The impact of the lectures was considerable and represented a serious loss of face for the government.

VII   Ortega and the Republic

The dictatorship was doomed and, pushed not only by the students and intellectuals, but also by the economic depression and the withdrawal of support by the king and the military, Primo de Rivera resigned his post and went into exile in France at the end of January 1930. Within weeks he was dead. Meanwhile, a simulacrum of political normalcy was established under General Dámaso Berenguer, whose government on February 1 restored Ortega and the other dissident professors to their posts. However, the republican fever was spreading rapidly, particularly among liberal intellectuals, and Ortega's own conversion may have come as early as the summer of 1930. In November he ended two articles with the phrase "*Delenda est Monarchia,*" recalling Cato's call, but when he used it a third time, on November 15, the king brought pressure to bear upon the owners of *El Sol* to remove Ortega from its pages. On February 10, 1931, one day after the lifting of censorship,[28] Ortega, Gregorio Marañón, and Ramón Pérez de Ayala published the manifesto of the Group at the Service of the Republic, which hoped to influence the municipal elections that had been called for April 12, preparatory to the parliamentary elections intended to reestablish constitutional democracy. Under the presidency of the poet Antonio Machado, the Group's first meeting was held on February 14, in Segovia.

Both Ortega's political stance and the change in ownership of *El Sol* made his continued collaboration there impossible, and on March 25 he and other collaborators left for *Crisol* [Crucible], a new paper also financed by Urgoiti, the first issue of which appeared on April 4. *Crisol* adhered to the principles of the Group at the Service of the

Republic, which, however, presented no candidates in the election. With the startling success of republican candidates on April 12 and the fall of the monarchy on April 14, the political and social life of Spain changed suddenly and dramatically and Ortega found himself completely dedicated to politics. General elections for a Constituent Parliament were called for June 28 and the Group won fourteen seats. Ortega was elected in both León and Jaén, but he resigned the latter seat. The work of the Constituent Parliament and the attitude of the Republican government quickly began to disappoint him, however, and he found that he had far less impact than he had hoped. The dominant figure in the government was Manuel Azaña, and between the two men there had always existed a mutual dislike. Whatever real political ambitions Ortega may have entertained were severely limited, although two of his ideas were incorporated into the new constitution: the idea of a "Republic of Workers" and the reaffirmation of a need for regional autonomy.

On July 31 Ortega was made a member of the Parliamentary Commission of State, which dealt with foreign relations, and he became chairman on August 11. Like Unamuno, he was mentioned from time to time as a possible candidate for the presidency of the Republic, but by the middle of November his disillusionment had grown to the point where there was a widespread belief that he planned to form yet another political party. At 11:30 A.M. on December 6, 1931, a group of invited guests, chosen by Ortega, collected in the Cine de la Opera to hear his address "Rectification of the Republic," which was broadcast by radio throughout the country. The speech was a harsh criticism of the politicians of the Republic, in which many detected a move to the right as Ortega singled out the Conservative Catholic Republican Miguel Maura for special praise.[29] In general, the reaction was negative, although Ortega's followers at *Crisol* and some Catholic groups praised him.

On January 7, 1932, *Luz, Diario de la República* [Light, Daily of the Republic] made its first appearance. It was to be Ortega's last and least successful attempt to create a sympathetic newspaper, but its conception was also less noble than that of his other publications. It lacked a strong financial base and declared itself to be in support of Azaña, in the futile hope that he would contribute to the paper's survival and join Ortega and Miguel Maura in the creation of new political party. The plan was rejected by all concerned.[30] This failure merely hardened Ortega's opposition to most of the Republicans, and in February he resigned as chairman of the Commission of State. The late spring of 1932 was dominated by the heated debate on the question of sovereignty and autonomy for Catalonia, a subject in which Ortega was deeply interested and on which he had much to say in Parliament. The importance of the debates forced him to cancel a trip to Berlin that had been planned for July. His stature was again damaged in August 1932, when he was widely suspected of having toyed with the idea of supporting General Sanjurjo's ill-fated uprising against the Republic in Seville. The final withdrawal came in October, when he dissolved the Group at the Service of the Republic.

The year was not completely disappointing, however, for in October he attended the celebration of the four hundredth anniversary of the founding of the University of Granada, and in November Espasa-Calpe published his collected works in a single volume. From this point on, Ortega was decidedly a writer for minorities, having been rejected as a political figure and deprived of a newspaper in which to publish his commentaries. He returned to theoretical essays and lectures which he published as soon as possible after they were delivered. His reputation abroad was still considerable, especially in Germany, where his attitudes were well received by the new regime. Ernst Robert Curtius did much to promote his work and his name appeared frequently in the prestigious *Europäische Revue* of Stuttgart. The summer of 1933 found him giving a course, "¿Qué es la técnica?" [What Is Technology?] at the new International University, in Santander.

He remained apart from all politics even though in October 1933 José Antonio Primo de Rivera, son of the late dictator and a great admirer of Ortega, founded, in the same theater where Ortega had delivered his speech on "Old and New Politics" in 1914, the Fascist Falange Española, which claimed to embrace many of Ortega's principles.[31] In April 1935 Ortega was awarded the Sash of the Republic, which he declined, but he did accept to be a guest, with Unamuno, at the opening of the Spanish House at the University City in Paris. In November, he published his last article in a Spanish newspaper. In March 1936 *El Sol* published special articles in honor of his twenty-five years at the University of Madrid, and later in the month he accepted the Gold Medal of the City of Madrid. The spring was spent in Holland, where he made a very successful lecture tour.

VIII   *Ortega in Exile*

In June 1936 Ortega suffered gall bladder problems and the outbreak of the Civil War found him ill at his home at 161, Calle Serrano.

Three days later he moved into the nearby Residencia de Estudiantes. Through the intervention of his brother Eduardo, a committed Republican and a member of the Madrid city council, he was issued a passport that allowed him to leave for France, ostensibly to undergo surgery. On August 30 Ortega and his family left Madrid for Alicante, where they took a French freighter to Marseilles. They settled in La Tronche, near Grenoble, until November, when they moved to a furnished apartment at 43, rue Gros, in Paris. As would be the case of many Spanish exiles, Ortega had lost everything except his reputation. His attitude toward the warring factions in Spain was part of his intimacy and remains so, although it is often assumed, on the basis of scanty evidence, that his sympathies lay with the Nationalists. Nevertheless, the day after his departure from Madrid, the monarchist newspaper *ABC* published a declaration of support for the Republic signed by Ortega, Marañón, Pérez de Ayala, Antonio Machado, Menéndez Pidal, and others, but Ortega later claimed that he had been bullied into allowing his name to appear.

Despite severe financial difficulties, he declined an invitation to teach at Harvard University, but in the spring of 1937 he was well enough to accept an invitation from Johann Huizinga to visit Holland. There he lived in "Het Witte Huis," within sight of the house that Descartes had once occupied in Oestgeest, near Leiden. He gave lectures in Rotterdam, Amsterdam, Delft, The Hague, and Leiden and, after two months, returned to France. Victoria Ocampo invited him to Argentina, but pleading the superiority of the libraries at his disposal in Paris, he declined. The winter of 1937–1938 seems to have been relatively happy for Ortega, and his essays written in Paris leave the impression of a man who had put much behind him. He spent the summer of 1938 in Saint-Jean-de-Luz, site of boyhood memories, and in the fall he returned to Paris. After a gall-bladder operation in October, he was moved to 11, rue Bassano, where he remained until late February 1939, when he moved to the south of Portugal. His mother died in Spain in April, and he spent part of the month of May in Vichy, before returning to Paris. He finally left for Argentina at the end of August, accompanied by his wife and daughter Soledad.

This final stay in Argentina was unlike the previous triumphal visits. Little interest was shown in his presence and he suffered frequent and lengthy bouts of nervous depression that caused him to abandon his plans for an extensive tour of South America, although he did manage short visits to Uruguay and Chile. His sister Rafaela died in November 1940. To many people, his political attitudes appeared to have become still more conservative, and after two and a half sad years in Buenos Aires he left in February 1942 to settle in Estoril, Portugal. There he founded a small publishing house, Editorial Azar, which published a single volume in 1943: a translation of Huizinga's *Homo Ludens*. In 1944 he gave a series of lectures at the University of Lisbon on the role of the intellectual and of intelligence.

IX   *The Exile Returns*

Ortega's first return to Spain since the outbreak of war took place in August 1945, when he acquired a small apartment at 11, Calle del Rey Francisco, in Madrid. He spent the rest of the summer in Zumaya and returned to Portugal for the winter. When the Madrid Ateneo reopened on May 4, 1946, Ortega delivered his talk "Idea del teatro" [The Idea of the Theater]. He was officially restored to his chair at the university, but he never taught there again. Nonetheless, he still carried within him the desire to influence the young and to contribute to the reestablishment of a normal cultural life in Spain after the upheavals and intransigence of the Civil War and its aftermath. His reintegration into Spanish life was, however, very gradual and impeded both by the hostility of the Church and the mistrust felt by the government of General Franco.

He spent the summers of 1946 and 1947 near San Sebastián, where he gave several lectures. In September 1947 he delivered a series of four lectures, "An Introduction to Velázquez," to the Royal Basque Society of Friends of the Country, and in the same year the Spanish Association for the Advancement of Science commemorated the tercentenary of the birth of Leibniz. Ortega's talk "Concerning Optimism in Leibniz" was the inaugural address. The summer of 1948 was spent at La Granja, near Segovia, and about this time he also acquired his final residence in Madrid at 28, Monte Esquinza.

The Franco regime did little to facilitate Ortega's life in Spain. He was refused permission to recommence publication of the *Revista de Occidente*, apparently because of the opposition of Franco himself, but in 1948 Ortega and his disciple Julián Marías were permitted to open the Instituto de Humanidades ("Institute of Humanities"), a sort of private school that began its short life in the Círculo Mercantil of Madrid. More successful than either Ortega or Marías had anticipated, Ortega's classes were soon moved to the Barceló Theater.[32] Notwithstanding its success, the school was ordered closed by the government in 1950. Ortega had failed to reassert his influence in Spain: the lack of opportunities to publish and speak freely kept him in isolation and an entire generation had grown up virtually ignorant of his work.

His last years were spent largely abroad, where he lectured and received many honors. In July 1949 he visited Aspen, Colorado, to attend a conference commemorating the bicentenary of the birth of Goethe, and in September he visited Germany for the same reason. He spoke in Hamburg, Berlin, Darmstadt, and Munich, where he was made a member of the Bavarian Academy of Fine Arts. On September 7, in the Free University of Berlin, he spoke on "*De Europa meditatio quaedam*," and attracted such an enthusiastic crowd that he had to be smuggled in and out of the building by the police. He spent the summer of 1950 at La Granja again, and in 1951 he returned to Germany. He spoke once more in Darmstadt, where he met Martin Heidegger, and he received an honorary doctorate of laws at Marburg.[33] He participated in the "Recontres Internationales" in Geneva and was awarded an honorary doctorate by the University of Glasgow.

The following year was unproductive, but in May 1953, at the age of seventy, he was officially retired from his chair by the Ministry of Education. He participated in a colloquium in London and once again returned to Germany, where his reputation had diminished somewhat, for many of his comments seemed tactless to his audiences, still traumatized by the war. As a result, a plan to bring him to the University of Munich as a guest professor failed, as did his own idea of a German branch of the Institute of Humanities that would have been established in Hamburg.[34] Nonetheless, he continued to publish extensively in German periodicals. His health kept him from accepting an invitation from the University of Puerto Rico, and from visiting Cuba and Venezuela. As he wrote to his brother Eduardo, who was then living in Cuba: "for years, I have been suffering periods of great depression that sometimes last for many months. It is because of circulatory problems, a sign of age."[35] He had become a greatly demoralized man, who seemed to have lost his sense of purpose.

Ortega spoke again in Munich and Württemburg in 1954, and also returned to Britain to speak in Torquay in October. His last lecture was given in Venice in May 1955, and most of the summer was spent in Asturias. In September, while at the farm of his son-in-law near Valladolid, he became ill and was taken back to Madrid where, on October 12, he underwent surgery for cancer. Upon his return to the apartment on Calle Monte Esquinza, he was visited by a Jesuit, Father Félix García, and the Archbishop of Zaragoza, of whose visits much was made by the press. Certain factions claimed, falsely, that Ortega had made a deathbed conversion.[36] On Tuesday, October 18, 1955, at 11:20 A.M. he died, surrounded by his wife, his brother Manuel, his three children, his daughters-in-law, and his son-in-law. A funeral mass was celebrated and he was buried in consecrated ground in a ceremony that attracted hundreds of students whose sudden sense of loss led to demonstrations that required the intervention of the police.

Ortega's final years had been ones of unhappy wandering. He himself saw his return to Spain as tentative and the cool and even hostile reception that he was accorded greatly disappointed him. Upon the death of Unamuno in 1936, Ortega had expressed a fear that Spain was about to enter a long period of silence. His own efforts to break it failed. For nearly twenty years, he was an exile both abroad and at home, victim of the "Jesuit conspiracy"[37] and government policy, as his integrity was repeatedly called into question. Nonetheless, his philosophical work had nurtured an important generation of thinkers and demonstrated that, as many have said, it was again possible to think in Spanish.

CHAPTER 2

Rationalism, Objectivism, and Phenomenology

I *The Two Generations*

AS with any socially aware thinker, the first fact of Ortega's life was the circumstance into which he was born: a time of political and intellectual expediency in which the lack of leadership in all aspects of national life had become accepted as natural. From his first article, Ortega demonstrated a conviction that it was up to his generation to serve as the instrument to bring about reform through awareness. Now generally known as the "Generation of 1914," it would consist of those Spaniards born in the 1880s, whose coming of age coincided with the disaster of 1898, who began to assume their place in national life at the outbreak of World War I, and who held the reins of power during the Second Republic. However, the difficulty of identifying the generation to which he belonged is shown by Ortega's initial tendency to associate himself with the younger members of the Generation of 1898. Such a self-perspective is understandable when one considers that the precocious Ortega began publishing in 1902, at almost the same time as many members of the older generation, from whom he naturally absorbed a deep concern for the situation of the country. They had helped to reduce the distance between Spain and modern Europe through their cultural and intellectual enthusiasm and their crusading instinct, and while their political effectiveness had been negligible, their personal independence and deep commitment to the very nature of the country had established a moral standard of a very high order. Although the young Ortega was greatly impressed by the political vision of Costa, and even the intellectual breadth of the conservative Menéndez Pelayo, both of them members of a still earlier generation, it was the spiritual leadership of Unamuno, the preeminent intellect in contemporary Spain, that would guide him until after his return from Germany. Unamuno

helped make his name known to the public in an article published in
1904, and for several years they maintained a correspondence in
which Unamuno's generous example made him a confessor for the
younger man. Only gradually did Ortega realize that they were
products of different times.

Turn-of-the-century Spain was full of chaos and recriminations that
Ortega could understand, but not share. In attempting to identify
those contemporaries who shared this bitter inheritance, he eventually came to feel that the previous generation, as a consequence of the
attitudes into which it had been born, could not avoid being a
historical failure:

1898 was the sudden annihilation of the history of Spain. . . . The generation
of 1898 found itself without a nation in which to fulfill itself or individuals
whom it could follow. It found itself without a house and without parents in
the spiritual order. It is a historically spurious generation. Not much can be
asked of it. It is a phantom generation. . . . It has had to reduce itself to the
most unreal form of life: it has lived theoretically; rather, critically.

Very well: I believe that it has thus completed the first part of its mission.
When it is not possible to do anything, the most that can be done is to
criticize, to analyze what others did. In this way the possibility of a new life is
prepared. (X, 226–27; 1913)[1]

The Generation of 1898 had, in many cases, foreseen the disintegration of the country and the disillusionment of their vital experience
was direct, whereas Ortega's generation was differentiated by having
been born into ruins. He hoped that its finest members would reveal
themselves by the time that they were thirty, and that they would
replace the Generation of 1898's mysticism with a strong sense of
discipline, but he recognized that the circumstances of their own
birth could have the opposite effect: "When one is born in a country
where nothing is right, sensitivity is dulled and we end up forgetting
that everything is wrong" (X, 106; 1909).

Clearly, the German experience had served to make clear not only
the definition of his own generation, but also to give Ortega his own
sense of a personal mission. In 1908 he publicly disagreed with
Menéndez Pelayo over the matter of lay education for Spain, and with
Maeztu over the relative superiority of men or ideas,[2] but the tower-
ing event of Ortega's early intellectual development came in 1909
when he made a conscious attempt to move out of the shadow of
Unamuno.[3] The excuse was the "europeanization" of Spain, but the
time had come when, both as an individual and as a member of a

historical generation, Ortega felt the need for independence and a sense of self. He and Unamuno held similar views on goals for Spain, but their approaches were becoming every more divergent. The guidance needed by Ortega's generation had to come from within and he called for "reflective moments, and for this are needed a plan and a direction. We beg those who can to offer them to us" (X, 112; 1909).

He urged his contemporaries to study and acquire the science and the European moral sensitivity to which he had been exposed. They must provide the impulse for new spiritual and social leadership, and as early as 1909[4] he spoke of the dynamic tension between the masses and a true aristocracy of qualified people that must be inherent in any true society. The leading figures of society must indeed be the best possible. Their superiority must spring from their private nature: the ideas, attitudes, and ability to evaluate that are the domain of the gifted individual. Through education and culture the people must be developed to take a role in the history of their country by aspiring to goals that will enrich the common future. Ortega revealed the neo-Kantian imprint by declaring: "The ideal that our people may have today does not matter to me; I care only about the one that they ought to have" (X, 44; 1908). His idealism considered politics the antithesis of the intellectual effort, since it rendered truth secondary to the need for swaying the masses, yet he hoped that a loftier, systematic form of politics could mean "an action upon the indeterminate will of the people" (X, 65; 1908). The mission of his generation lay in making culture and politics one.

II   *Liberalism and Socialism*

In line with the traditions of his family and his class, Ortega considered himself a liberal, and by 1906, all but overwhelmed by the promise of science during his studies in Germany, he declared his own liberalism to be socialistic. Deeply influenced by the thought of Paul Natorp and by the example of Unamuno,[5] Ortega considered socialism to be the rigorous application to politics of the cultural values that he had absorbed in Germany. He dismissed political conservatism as nothing more than a base instinct, while envisioning liberalism as "magnanimous politics" (X, 169; 1910), the system that allowed freedom to both its enemies and its friends. He insisted that liberalism was revolutionary by definition, standing for necessary change and always recognizing the essentially temporary nature of any form of government or system of laws. It was the conscience of a nation's political life, a cultural force, an emotion, a duty, a mission and a trust, but never a convenience. More important, such emphasis on ideals would shift political pressures from the rigid limitations of written laws to the vitality of society's constantly evolving structures. However, a new liberal party could be born only after the values were resuscitated in a stimulating cultural medium where natural forces could be brought under man's ethical and rational control.

Such deep-rooted conviction of moral purpose would lead in the direction of full and free participation in the spiritual development of the nation, but the protection of individual freedom must be accompanied by an obligation of the State to help the individual learn to use his liberty effectively. Ortega thus saw in liberalism the natural home for young intellectuals, since they would be especially well qualified to achieve these pedagogical goals, and he declared it to be their social duty since "Spain, the organization of Spain, will be liberal or it will continue not to be" (X, 167; 1910). No other attitude could involve a sufficiently broad range of the citizenry.

Although he never became a member of the Spanish Socialist party, for Ortega socialism was a way of being European. It added to liberalism a systematic program that transcended petty nationalisms by aiming to bring together various countries in common goals. It was the *means* of restoring the liberal philosophy to European, and especially Spanish, politics, and with some finality he stated: "today no liberalism is possible other than socialist liberalism" (X, 37; 1908). In 1908 and 1909 he declared that socialism was obliged to defend and indeed establish cultural and moral values in the face of the two major enemies confronting Spain: "the ignorance of the citizen and the astuteness of the priest" (X, 87; 1908), but he did not agree with the party that it should enter into open conflict with the Church. Rather, it should take the high road and exemplify the energy and strength of the new values, to show that virtue could also be a lay product.

Ortega spent most of 1911 in Germany again, and upon his return he saw the Spanish Socialist Party as merely the visible tip of theoretical socialism. It had taken root among the workers, but unlike socialism in Germany and England, it had attracted scant support among intellectuals. He came to see that it was no longer possible for intellectuals to be merely socialists: the *prágmata* of socialism had evolved into a rather inflexible form, while the socialism of most intellectuals, however intense, was inevitably associated with other ideas as well. The difficulty was that the Socialist party was prepared to accept only those who believed in the completeness of the doctrine.

The modification in Ortega's attitude does not reveal a genuine disillusionment with socialism. In fact, until 1913, the source of his discomfort was rather a question of the techniques needed to bring about the changes that he desired, and his own role and responsibility within the mechanism. His growing intellectual independence and public authority made it increasingly difficult for him to resolve effectively the dualism of a philosophical and a socially active stance. Nonetheless, he was constant in his insistence that there were strong links between socialism and the rise of a new aristocracy. Instead of the capitalist system of economic classes defined by the impersonal power of money, he believed that socialism would divide men into better and worse, on the basis of their competency and such cultural and spiritual values as "Art, Science, Refinement, Moral Energy" (X, 240; 1913). Whereas capitalism makes true aristocracies impossible, socialism makes them indispensable. Given the relative poverty of all of Spain's social classes, the solution to her problems lay less in the class struggle than in the moral perfection of her citizens through scientific discipline. For this reason, he could not declare himself a true Marxist.

Ortega's gradual drift away from the party was due also to his perception that it was unrealistic in its approach to the international ramifications of the movement. International socialism had evolved according to the characteristics of such industrially advanced countries as England and Germany. Undeniably, their experience offered models, but Spanish socialism had first to deal with the unique Spanish reality: "socialist parties have to be all the more national as their respective nations are less built up" (X, 206, 1912). In a barely industrialized nation, where nearly two-thirds of the citizens were illiterate, the struggle to better the lot of the workers could have meaning only once an effective, although not necessarily satisfactory, social system was in place: "The day that Spanish workers abandon abstract words and recognize that they are suffering, not just as proletarians, but also as Spaniards, they will make the Socialist party the strongest in Spain. In the process, they will make Spain. This will be the nationalization of socialism. . . . The international does not exclude the national, it includes it" (X, 206; 1912).

III *The Education of a Nation*

Sophisticated awareness of foreign achievements would lead to the creation of a truly Spanish culture and spirit which, Ortega suspected, may never have existed, despite the ravings of entrenched traditionalists. Repeatedly he demanded nothing less than a Spanish interpretation of the world, but this required a degree of cultural development that could turn Europe into the high peak from which Spain could contemplate the contributions that she could make in her own right: "Spain is a European possibility. Only seen from Europe is Spain possible" (I, 138; 1910). Europe meant science, and to raise Spain out of the world's intellectual slums, torrential inundations of world knowledge were needed to soften both the heads and the lands of the peninsula. Science represented all the elements lacking in the Spanish character: discipline, a sense of system, a sense of priorities, and, above all, precision. It was a truly contemporary mode that came to fill the void left by the dissipation of traditional religious faith. Scientific inquiry could discipline the irrational forces that Spain had always allowed to run rampant. Spain's idea of science was of a small private activity without social aims, but Ortega believed that a country that had not a single modern scientific library had absolutely no guarantee of survival.[6] Contemporary accomplishments abroad were largely the result of advanced technology, which Ortega recognized as perhaps the outstanding development of the twentieth century. Yet, in all parts of national life, Spain scorned technical expertise; she was unique in Europe in her casual disregard for the enduring effects of such a lack of skills. In a sense, Ortega's early goals were summed up when he commented: "A new Spain is possible only if these two terms are united: democracy and competence. The restoration of democracy is possible in Spain only by means of the revolution of competence" (X, 231; 1913).

Both science and technology were for Ortega the fruits of culture, which, after Marburg, he saw as human life dedicated to the harnessing of natural forces, the interplay and exchange of points of view across both space and time. On the other hand, civilization was the totality of means, applied culture, and could be imported or counterfeited. Uninterested in the problems set forth by the intellectual and spiritual activities of concerned man, Spain had substituted the established and finally static pattern of civilization for the activity, stimulation, and anguish of a culture that gives it life. Ortega believed that the challenging and problematic character of culture is inspired by an almost religious aspiration to surpass mere necessity and to dedicate oneself to the apparently superfluous, and he considered this to be a fundamental quality of man, an essential definition of his humanness. The results are uncertain, but only in such searches can man hope to situate and surpass himself.

Elaborating at first the thought of Nietzsche, Ortega called culture the truly human impulse, but he soon went beyond Nietzsche in his demand that the responsible minority be the energizing force. For the young Ortega, culture was virtue and "an act of kindness more than of genius" (X, 77; 1908). Later, in the glow of neo-Kantianism, culture was seen as the supreme social enterprise and a unifying force within and between societies. He believed that culture conquers the rudeness of natural life, which in mankind is aggression, and creates an air of peace and friendship. It is man at his best, a series of conventions that raise him above the beast by helping him to know what to expect from life and thereby treat his fellow man with ease and confidence.

The young Ortega rejected the uncontrolled passion and inarticulate impulse of primitive man that he detected beneath the skin of contemporary Spanish civilization and declared that "the State has a primary duty, culture, [and] a primary crime, the ignorance of its members" (X, 58; 1908). He urged that the government take steps to revitalize the universities and bring to Spain those outstanding Europeans who set standards. In her isolation Spain had no standards with which to compare herself, and the resulting complacency threatened her very survival. Just as Germany had first received her vitality upon absorbing Latin culture, so now must Spain use German science as a starting point for the creation of new passions and new ideas.[7]

Repeatedly he insisted that education was the key to the salvation of Spain. Notwithstanding the advances brought about by Krausism and the Institución Libre de Enseñanza, in political terms such progress had resolved itself into a tangle of inadequate legislation that he condemned as a national scandal (X, 197; 1912). Too much emphasis was given, he said, to the secularization of education, an idea that he supported, but that distracted people's attention from the real need, which was for more imaginative innovations in education, taking into consideration culture and political responsibility. He gave systematic form to his conviction in 1910 when he spoke before the society "El Sitio" in Bilbao. His speech, "Social Pedagogy as a Political Program," was an attempt to draw into a coherent social program his various concerns for national renewal. By his own admission, his presentation owed much to the thought of one of his professors in Marburg, Paul Natorp, yet it was also a significant step in the formulation of Ortega's own ideas.

Since education converts imperfect, rude man into a potent creature, full of reverberations, he pointed out the need for a vision of what man must be so that education may be able to develop the tools to permit him to reach that fulfillment, yet as an integral ingredient of his community and society, not as an abstract unit, torn out of his circumstance. The transformation of Spanish society required that politics take upon itself the task of educating the people for a new social order in which the cultural tradition is reestablished by the directing classes and men sense the community of their efforts. We must, he said, save ourselves in things, which are the results of our labors: "A group of men who work on a common job receive in their hearts, by reflection, the unity of that job, and unanimity is born among them. A true community or society is founded upon the unanimity of work" (I, 517; 1910). Maintaining that socialism was the only system that was morally admissible, Ortega declared that if each citizen is expected to contribute to culture, he is also entitled to be provided with a cultural consciousness. This is the role of education through lay schools, free from the restrictions of the Church and the family: "society is the only educator, as society is the only end of education" (I, 519).[8]

IV *The League for Political Education*

After a decade of journalism dedicated to the analysis of the Spain in which he found himself, Ortega turned in 1913 and 1914 to the creation of the Liga de Educación Política ("League for Political Education"), which represented the putting into practice of his social ideas. Composed of ninety-eight members from the intellectual and professional classes, the league was, as Ortega intended, and despite the presence of some older men, the first public action of those men in their thirties who would soon become the effective rulers of Spain. In his speech "Vieja y nueva política" [Old and New Politics],[9] which served to inaugurate the league, he pointed to the division of Spain into two camps: "official Spain," the political and social usages of the Restoration that still held sway in the country; and "vital Spain," including the younger generation whose undeveloped energies led them to feel no identification with the corrupt old standards. Instead of the healthy interchange of forces between governed and governors that causes the social processes to reflect the changing needs and nature of the country, official Spain had become rigid and unresponsive, as politics had become a lucrative profession devoted to selfish interests. Ortega recognized that the seriousness of this lay not in the *abuses* that such a system inflicted upon an innocent populace, but rather in the *uses*, the procedures that, however immoral, become accepted as part of the system. The race was diseased and no levels of the national infrastructure inspired respect or loyalty: "Official Spain consists, then, of sort of phantom parties that defend the phantom of a few ideas and that, supported by the shadows of a few newspapers, cause a few hallucinatory ministries to function" (I, 274; 1914).

In contrast, the league was to be the organ for "another aspiring, germinal Spain, *a vital Spain*, perhaps not very strong, but vital, sincere, honorable, which, hindered by the other one, does not manage to enter fully into history" (I, 273). This new element was not defined by a class or profession, but by an attitude, a level of cultural awareness, and a renewed set of criteria that Ortega hoped would define and characterize the entire younger generation. Although the league claimed no interest in becoming another political party intent upon gaining power, Ortega made clear that there existed in Spain no other social instrument of sufficient authority to bring together a large group of people with similar ideals without political intervention. The scope of the movement was national but not, as he was quick to point out, nationalistic: rather than desire a return to an imperialistic Spain, the League wanted simply "a Spain in good health, nothing more than a vertebrate and upright Spain" (I, 299).[10] The achievement of these general goals was to be carried out by means of propaganda that would aim to create means of greater social cohesion, enriched culture, technology, and public energy through the disciplined marshaling of will in broad social groups. It could not be assumed that the state was capable of developing a fertile and stimulating atmosphere, but it, along with all the other organs of the nation, must be imbued with a new dynamism, for only in relation to the other does either part fulfill its potential.

Ortega emphatically declared that the league would have nothing to do with existing political factions. The Liberals and Conservatives were the Restoration incarnate and the principal enemies of the movement. Republicanism had not yet displayed its usefulness, and the league would support the monarchy only because the spirit of the country was still monarchist, and insofar as the monarchy could constantly justify itself and become again an integral part of the nation. The Socialist and Syndicalist movements were the only modern forces in Spanish public life and shared many ideals with the league, but Ortega rejected their doctrinairism. The league would be democratic and broadly liberal, but without dogma. Above all, it aimed to create a new political constituency that could not be served by the old divisions between Left and Right.

There were two means by which Ortega felt this social breadth could be achieved. Society needed the leadership of the most competent, and for this reason the league made its appeal especially to the professional and intellectual classes. The highly trained groups could not only use their skills to revitalize and reform the social mechanisms, but could also transmit their professional enthusiasm in the hopes of pulling the masses out of their indolence. The second means of reaching all levels of Spanish society was through decentralization of Spanish life. Government after government had seen Madrid as the totality of the country, until the provinces had effectively ceased to exist both politically and socially. Ortega would develop and systematize this idea later, but already the basic forces were in play; he wished Madrid to be considered simply as a more highly developed province whose duty it would be "To spur on to a life of their own the weaker provinces and pick up, from those who have awakened, teachings, suggestions and emulations" (I, 305). Ortega's address was too much like a university lecture, his concepts were often ambiguous, his tone was patronizing, his rhetorical style seduced without convincing and the league soon disappeared. Its ideas, however, were the orientation behind the new review that Ortega helped to found, logically called *España*.

V   *The Search for Standards*

Preceding the influence of German cultural discipline in Ortega's formation was a debt to French Romanticism, and particularly to Chateaubriand, Victor Hugo, and Hippolyte Taine, that provided an example of style and personal emotion which remained with him throughout his life. As he admitted in 1934, "I owe much, much to France" (VIII, 22). The young Ortega was especially attracted by the attitudes of the cultural historian Ernest Renan, with whom he identified and whose religious stance probably affected his own.[11] Particularly appealing was the belief in man as a progressive creature, ever moving towards greater unity as the historical legacy of culture gradually enriched the harsher, lower, levels of his being. Ortega felt close to Renan, whose entire life he saw as a "zig-zag" between scientific exactitude and aesthetic delight. He felt that Renan had succeeded in reconciling the apparently opposed demands of the objective and subjective worlds into "the world of the credible" (I, 451; 1909), a world made of harmony itself and that provided the stuff of "art and religion, poetry and myth, with the limitless richness of their forms" (I, 453). Renan's new world was "the same as that of real things submitted to a peculiar interpretation: the metaphorical" (I, 454). Ortega saw the creation of metaphors as a means of bringing together and uniting apparently disparate things in an unrestricted enrichment of life. He had acquired a faith in culture as a unifying power that represents that body of points on which the greatest number of men come together, an agreement rooted in intrahuman factors, a sort of irony through which men may commune.

Ortega himself still scorned "the secret leprosy of subjectivity, of the individual ego" (I, 477), and insisted on objective truth and the immutability of things as instruments to refine man's admirative scale. Such a stand was, as he said, a search for some guide beyond the perishability of man; a search for standards, systems and a hierarchy that were unchanging. Following both Renan and Marburg, he was drawn to classicism as "a testimony of the ideal unity of man" (I, 458) and believed that a return to classical norms could offset the drift and chaos of modern society, by restoring its sense of the intrinsic harmony of life and the need to surpass oneself in search of sure and lasting ideals.

Such standards could be of particular benefit, he believed, in the crisis in the arts that cast an ominous pall over an essential aspect of human activity. Ortega saw art as a serious undertaking that must have one foot in reality and the other in regions hitherto unknown in the human landscape. All art, like philosophy and life itself, is a treatment of an insoluble problem symbolized by the artist in a small scrap of reality that, when carried to its final power, serves to express the entire world (I, 464). In "Adán en el Paraíso" [Adam in Paradise], however, written between May and August 1910, his disenchantment with the rigid norms of idealism began to become evident. He used painting to demonstrate the transcendental quality of artistic creation, made up, it is true, in terms of both depiction and materials, of things, but unique in that it creates something that is not a thing, a unit that is not found in nature: the picture itself as art. The essence lies in the relationship between things, each one of which is a series of relationships given its being by the limitations imposed upon it by other things. Ortega no longer spoke of aggressiveness, yet its underlying importance is indisputable. Convincingly, he declared that things *are* values and relationships. Moving away from his claim that subjectivity is error, he recognized that for each man that which is apparently the same is in fact different and that there are as many realities as there are points of view, as fundamental a concept for artistic creativity as for his own theories of perspectivism.

As his philosophy became more absorbent, he demonstrated that science and ethics, in which laws are the determining factor, and art, in which they are merely indicators, are all indispensable to the solution of the "heroic, tragic problem" that each man carries within; only art and the subjectivity that aspires to objectivity can hope to solve the "last corner of the problem" (I, 479). By indicating which aspects of the human problem are being resolved by science and ethics, it becomes possible to isolate the problem of art, the prime characteristic of which is insolubility. Such awareness is a divine attribute to which all men aspire. Adam was merely the first for whom life was a problem, the first who had to deal with the things he found in Paradise and learn how to manage both the limits and the opportunities they offered to the problem that is life, but every man, in his individual circumstance, relives this need for orientation.[12]

Some of his ideological abstractions fell away as Ortega saw that each thing *is* in the measure that it is either for an individual or for another thing, and that "the essence of each thing resolves itself in pure relationships" (I, 481). Just as things *are* for man, so *is* man for things. Whereas science's field of inquiry is commonness, those abstract relationships that transcend individuals and are necessarily not vital, art is a method that goes beyond and realizes, individualizes and potentiates things in a "new world of pure vitality" (I, 483). Supreme works of art are far more than the sum of the things that are their parts, and reveal to us all relationships, an entire world; through them, suddenly, "we have been raised to an intuition superior to the human" (I, 484). To make real the thing that the artist aims to produce is to copy not the thing itself, but the idea of it, yet to do so, he must depend on and conquer reality. Quite unlike the scientist who must split life into the world of nature and the world of the spirit, the artist begins in one of these worlds and moves toward the other.

Ortega saw the essence of European art as the product of the contrasting characters of the Continent's two main types of man: Mediterranean and Gothic, an idea he pursued in "Arte de este mundo y del otro" [Art of This World and of the Other, 1911]. Since the time of the caves of Altamira, and through the "honorable weightiness" (I, 189) of Romanesque art, Mediterranean man had revealed a powerful artistic will that was the result of his unique closeness to the earth and the tangible, fed by "an underground current that looks for the trivial, the intranscendental" (I, 200). In contrast, northern, Gothic man, in his great cathedrals, displayed an aspiration away from this world which resolved itself into ascending, soaring lines, a transcendence indicative of "a desire to lose oneself in a mobility that is potentiated antinaturally; a supersensitive and spiritual mobility, thanks to which our soul is freed of the feeling of being subject to what is real" (I, 204). Mediterranean art was sensual and impressionistic, while northern art was more profound and conceptual. This contrast was all but resolved in the aspiration to synthesis found in Renaissance art in which the artist sought natural harmony and inner vitality through the assiduous study of real forms. In recent years, however, painting had fallen into a stasis and misapprehension of values as too much attention was paid to technique. [13] Ortega was to argue forcefully that the nineteenth-century concept of beauty as a utilitarian and orderly instinct had to be surpassed by new norms, and herein lay mission of aesthetics and all forms of criticism, which he saw as necessary adjuncts to the creative process.

He believed that serious literary criticism, for example, was "an ennobling, although it may be provisional, of that which is in crisis" (I, 159; 1910). It was a leading of the common reader to the light, with the conviction that criticism could enrich art and literature much as philosophy could enhance life: "I seem to perceive the mission of criticism as a disintegration of the elements of a work with the purpose of potentiating them, carrying them to maximum growth so that, upon rereading the book, all its inner energies seem multiplied. Like the varnish on a picture, criticism aspires to endow literary objects with a purer atmosphere, an atmosphere of high mountain air, where the colors are more alive and the perspective broader" (IX, 479; 1914?). The bourgeois ethic of the nineteenth century had dealt a near death blow to artistic authenticity and Ortega confessed that his most frequent reaction to contemporary Spanish books, for example, was "a heaviness in my heart and a spiritual dryness in my soul" (I, 45; 1906), such that any vitality he could discern was encouraging. He held firm in his belief that it was in the great artistic and intellectual figures that man could find examples of his own potential and hope for his own success: "Only because Plato, Cervantes and Saint Francis of Assisi lived have we come to believe that our lineage is neither idiotic nor egotistical" (I, 163; 1910).

Responsible criticism must stimulate high standards, and he summed up the most rudimentary requirements for any book when he declared: "So, what is a book? What a man makes when he has a style and sees a problem. Without one and without the other there is no book. Deprived of a style, a book is a rough draft, printed paper. The problem is the guts of the book. For that reason the only ones that live with a life of their own are those within which throbs a problem

that really is a problem" (I, 240; 1914). Such qualities were characteristic of the works of most members of the Generation of 1898, but
not always of the writers most in vogue. Despite his ambivalent
reaction to the Generation as a group, Ortega showed repeated
interest in many of its individual members and attempted to discern
in their works indications of fruitful tendencies that might be developed. He saw in their nonconformity a rejection of the myths of
nineteenth-century Spain and an ardent desire to build a new, authentic Spain from scratch. Their prickly personalities and frantic
viewpoints notwithstanding, Ortega recognized that "those who have
something to say know very well how much they owe to those
barbaric Hercules who took upon themselves the uttering of certain
great and elementary atrocities that necessarily had to be said" (IX,
496; 1914?). Indeed, they were each a style and displayed a force of
will that was rare in Spain, yet their message went largely unheeded.

More disturbing was that he saw in the younger writers a willful
ignorance of the state of mind of the moment in which they were
writing. Although he admitted that "reading verses is not one of my
habitual occupations" (VI, 248; 1914), it was here that the new trends
could be seen. He detected, however, an excessive influence of
Decadentism and was disturbed by the tendency of younger poets to
rely too much on the relationship between word sounds and music.
Like Unamuno, he was suspicious of such willingness to strip words of
their full ideological and semantic richness. He insisted that, as in the
case of painting, the materials employed must be their own transcendence and free themselves from their materiality as well as that of
the subject treated: "the distinctive feature of high poetry consists of
living from itself, of not needing land on which to support itself" (II,
124; 1910). The decadent trend in poetry was not unlike the drift
toward rhetoric and orientation that he found in prose.

Again he insisted that technique, regardless of how dazzling and
skillful, was only the outer shell and he wisely counseled his readers:
"let us reserve our love as readers for real poets, that is, for the men
who bring a new style, who are a style. Because these men enrich the
world, they augment reality" (VI, 247; 1914). Style is perspective and
is the peculiar way that a true artist converts observed reality into
poetry without destroying the reality of the thing itself. The unique-
ness of all authentic style is that it is inevitable, dictated by experience or observation and passed through the filter of artistic
individuality.

A demonstration of this dynamism that Ortega felt had to exist
between criticism and creativity can be found in the three shrewd

analyses that he devoted to the novels of Pío Baroja, in whom he perceived many of the characteristic attitudes of contemporary Spain, as expressed in her indigenous genre. In 1910 he wrote, had printed, but did not publish "Una primera vista sobre Baroja" [A First Look at Baroja]. Some time after the publication in 1911 of *El árbol de la ciencia* [The Tree of Knowledge], he wrote "Pío Baroja: anatomía de un alma dispersa" [Pío Baroja: Anatomy of a Scattered Soul]. "Ideas sobre Pío Baroja" [Ideas about Pío Baroja], published in the first volume of *El Espectador* in 1916, was probably written in 1915.[14] Less occasional in nature than the criticisms devoted to other contemporaries, these remain among the most penetrating analyses of the mind and the novelistic art of Baroja.

Ortega believed that Baroja revealed important areas of weakness that were symptomatic of Spanish intellectual life at large, but that could be remedied in later novels, with the help of astute criticism. As he observed, "if literary criticism existed in Spain, Baroja would long ago have found a corrective that would perhaps have avoided certain grave defects in his production" (II, 93; 1915). It was the very personality of Baroja that defined his novels and that Ortega used as a background for his analyses. Baroja's intellectual independence moved him to write, not for aesthetic reasons, but rather to give form to an irritation at the society in which he found himself: the Spain of 1898, decadent, ruined, and yet insensitive to her plight. Ortega predicted that the enduring importance of his books would lie in their value as "national symptoms" of a desire to rise towards a new way of life (II, 111; 1910). Herein lay, however, one of the weaknesses that Ortega considered characteristically Spanish: the very criticism itself was enjoyable to Baroja, yet ultimately ineffective, and it was this fascination with the farcical nature of his society that led Baroja to admire the savage and spontaneous aspects of man within civilization. Ortega condemned this vision as animalistic and artistically unworthy, but found it consistent with Baroja's hatred of the hypocrisy that led to a systematic perversion of man's natural scale of values. Indeed, Baroja found the entire world wanting and made this all-encompassing rejection the very center of his art. Ortega attributed this to his essentially timid and defensive nature that sprang from a feeling of frustration at his own impotence and that demanded the elimination of everyone else. Only an appealing streak of sentimentalism mitigated this.

Ortega saw in the Basque novelist an emotional rather than a logical writer. Since happiness for him was activity, but totally unshackled, Baroja often saw things more as a metaphysical writer than as a conventional novelist. His belief in the value of action was the dream of a man trapped by his society and unable to transform it artistically. Ortega found most of his characters perplexing and considered the vagabonds to be the most nearly successful creations since they represented an appropriate admixture of social isolation and dynamism, well suited to Baroja's vision of man as a failure. Ortega pointed out that this "Homer of the riff-raff" (II, 124; 1910), while presenting such characters as practical failures, did not see them as victims, but rather as moral and sentimental victors whose will was triumphant. They shared "the barbarous energy of men who split the crust of society in order to reach fresh air" (II, 113; 1910). Such strenuous rejection of external constraints was often called nihilism, but if that is true, said Ortega, "then nihilism is the sublime attitude: to feel what one feels and not what they tell us to feel" (II, 101; 1915). Baroja's intellectual and artistic independence was sincerity itself and this was what he seemed to require of man.

Baroja's technique was too impressionistic, based upon his own opinions of his characters, rather than upon allowing them to create and set forth their own reality. The author becomes more interesting than the novel itself. Despite Baroja's admiration for action, Ortega noted that, in fact, his characters are given to excessive talking and ratiocination. Moreover, although one of his greatest talents was the creation of vast numbers of characters, they tend to be excessively allusive, leaving the reader confused, his mind filled with the sensation of "countless characters who did a pirouette, dealt briefly with each other and then disppeared through the trapdoor" (II, 96; 1915). Baroja seemed unable to create a living medium in which his characters could develop their personalities. Because they seemed to have little interest in what happened to them, the reader could scarcely feel otherwise.

The result is novels that are violent, dark, and aggressive, leading Ortega to conclude that "Baroja is an exemplary phenomenon of the contemporary Spanish soul" (IX, 477; 1914). His works lacked the contemplative quality, the inner tension necessary for a truly great novel. Ortega rejected Baroja's idea that, since life is absurd and arbitrary, it was acceptable for the depiction of it also to lack both sense and structure. This simply gave the books a "stammering" characteristic,[15] a direct reflection not only of the author's own confusion, but also of his sincerity and lack of rhetoric. Ortega's belief that Baroja was a great writer who had not produced a masterpiece penetrated all three articles, yet he doubted that he would ever fulfill himself: "Baroja is nothing, and I presume he will never be anything" (II, 101; 1915). The state of artistic appreciation in Spain provided no pressures to discipline his art and tame its savage vitality.

VI   *The Philosophical Mission*

Into this desolate intellectual landscape Ortega tried to bring philosophy, broadly understood and presented in a fashion that could permit it to have a concrete effect upon the Spanish way of thinking and make Spain modern in the process. He aimed to overwhelm his compatriots with all that was newest in the most philosophically advanced nations of the West. In the years preceding World War I, that meant Germany. At first, his writings reveal the neo-Kantian idealism that he had been taught in Marburg, but as early as 1912,[16] he went further as he began to study seriously Edmund Husserl's theories of phenomenology. Almost immediately upon the publication in 1913 of Husserl's *Ideen zu einer reinen Phänomenologie,* Ortega produced at least three articles in which he brought some facets of these ideas to the attention of his countrymen. "Sensación, construcción e intuición" [Sensation, Construction and Intuition] and "Sobre el concepto de sensación" [On the Concept of Sensation], both published in 1913, show the attraction that the Husserlian theories held for him, but "Ensayo de estética a manera de prólogo" [An Essay on Aesthetics by Way of Prologue], published in 1914, shows Ortega already freeing himself of some of the limitations of phenomenology and establishing a philosophy that was at once useful to him and transmissible to his public.

In "On the Concept of Sensation," a discussion of a book by Heinrich Hoffmann, he offered a careful examination of the essence of phenomenology, which, much to his dismay, was still being confused with descriptive psychology. The central difficulty that he perceived in separating the two was the use of the term "human consciousness" to which each science laid claim. He felt that it was a combination of words too freighted with divergent meanings to be accurate, and preferred to speak instead of "consciousness of," when the being of objects is constituted, and in which the essence of all things has an absolute and immutable life, before and beyond being either real or unreal. Consciousness itself is not a reality, and Ortega insisted on distinguishing the proper study of explicative psychology, which is the contents of consciousness, from that of phenomenology, which is

Erlebnis, the mind's identification with its own feelings. Perception, however, may not be as simple as it seems, for although we perceive, for example, physical objects as being full, the senses reveal at any time only the surfaces. Therefore, perception is a synthesis of the consciousness of surface and that in which we make reference to the interior.

In the case of sight, a "real visual thing" is an inexhaustible series of perspectives with certain continuity that show us the permanence of the same object. None of the views can claim to be the real one, but only a presentation of a "visual thing" (*Sehding*). Many things that we see are not real, but ideal. For example, size. According to its distance from us, every real thing reveals various sizes to the viewer, yet he chooses one as the norm, what Hoffmann called the "natural size." Ortega pointed out that the natural size for the parts of a whole is not necessarily the same as for the whole, nor is the natural size of the whole necessarily the aggregate of the natural sizes of the parts because the "zone of distance" for each is different. Ortega's reservations at this point seem to rest on phenomenology's inability to provide an adequate theory for knowledge of the real.

In 1914, in his "Ensayo de estética a manera de prólogo," he developed more forcefully his reservations regarding Husserl's phenomenology. Although it is a frequently unclear work, it is an important step both in his attitude towards phenomenology and in the development of his aesthetics. He began by affirming the executant quality of the I and declaring that the I *is* insofar as it is being and acting itself from within. To become an object of contemplation it would have to be looked at from outside, at which point it would cease to be an I. Ortega's working assertion was: "Everything, looked at from within itself, is an *I*" (VI, 252), a concept that will also shed light on his later biographical approach to historiography. Everything seen from without is but an image *of*, or concept *of* something, but not that thing as an I. Thus our intelligence alone can understand only this external aspect and can never capture the intimacy of things. The aesthetic object, however, differs in that it possesses a transparency that seems to allow us to perceive the executant quality of its intimacy, from which we derive aesthetic pleasure. Art makes real the executant I.

Ortega's premise was that true poets are creators in that they expand reality through the creation of new things, an assertion that led him to investigate the nature of the metaphor, "the elementary aesthetic object, the beautiful all" (VI, 257). He discarded the conventional view that the metaphor is based upon similarity, contending instead that this is nothing more than the first step in the process. The metaphor stresses the fact that, despite and because of the similarities between the elements, they are not in fact the same. The awareness of this lack of sameness leads to the creation of a new object in which the "reality" of the original elements is destroyed; the new object that the poet has given us is possible only in another world. The reader witnesses the metaphor in its becoming; he witnesses its executant quality as it takes place within his own intimacy. The objective image given us by the poet produces a subjective reaction, "the very act of perception" (VI, 260), a phenomenon beyond intellection that is an integral part of the newly created object. Language is allusion to things, but art brings them into being; it is "executant expression" (VI, 262). Already, then, life, for Ortega, precedes consciousness.[17]

VII   "Meditations on Quixote"

With the publication in 1914 of *Meditaciones del Quijote*, Ortega established himself as an independent thinker and the leading representative of a new generation and a new attitude in Spain. The *Meditations* are only the first part of a projected study, which itself was to be only the first of ten meditations on a variety of themes that would, in some measure, refer to Spanish circumstances. Part of the study on Baroja, of course, was done, and one can assume that some of what Ortega was to write about Azorín in 1916[18] was intended for the projected meditation, but the others exist only as titles. As he approached his intellectual maturity, Ortega showed a growing sense of the need to build larger systems in which to place immediate problems.

The intention was to look at *Don Quixote* as an essential "circumstance" of Spain. There was no question of conventional literary criticism, but rather an attempt to solve the problem of Spanish destiny. *Don Quixote* represents perhaps the only case of Spanish fulfillment, but the secret is not a matter of plot or style, but lies rather in what the novel seems to conceal: a philosophy, a point of view, that is the ethic of a race, carried to its maximum power. It is the book in which one can attempt to find the Spain that could have been, and, by extension, a lesson that might still serve to answer in the twentieth century "the great question: my God, what is Spain?" (I, 360). The absence of the last two sections, "How did Miguel de

Cervantes see the world?" and "The Halcyonism of Cervantes," is strongly felt by the reader, who reaches the end of the existing essays, his appetite whetted and prepared to tackle the problems suggested. Nevertheless, as Marías says, we do have in our hands a highly provocative work that is in fact three things: a concrete book, a philosophical doctrine, and a historical action aimed at the creation of a new Spain.[19] Moreover, although the shadows of Marburg, Scheler, and others hang over it,[20] the book represents the moment when Ortega laid claim to a parcel of the history of Spanish thought as he strove to make his compatriots in general and his contemporaries in particular participate in an elegant reappraisal of the country's past and present. As he said some twenty years later, "the rest of my output, which was going to be a ceaseless battle against utopianism, is, then, already preformed in this first book of mine" (VIII, 44; 1934).

In the lengthy introduction, Ortega explained his purpose: to examine each subject in such a way that it would be raised to its fullest significance and set in a context in which it and everything around it would grow in intensity. Thus, from the first paragraphs, two of the principal aspects of the book become evident: the continuing importance of relationships; and the value of love, the Platonic *amor intellectualis*, as a force for understanding and appreciation that finds the potential fulfillment that is inherent in everything, however small, and weaves it into "the elemental currents of the spirit, basic human preoccupations" (I, 312). The *Meditations* have as their core Cervantes's novel, which is the product of the man and his circumstance, a coming to grips with his objective, primary world. A dispassionate effort to understand how this occurs will help the reader to understand his own circumstance, contemporary Spain, and prepare him for the fulfillment of both his own destiny and that of his country by carrying the circumstance to its full power in a genuine desire to comprehend, to include. Love is an enrichment of both subject and object and demands the creation of links and structures that relate individuals, however briefly, with the object of their attention. The example of this book would contrast with the hatred and exclusiveness that Ortega believed had so long contributed to the "rigid, dry, sordid and deserted" (I, 312) character of the Spanish universe, devoid of a sense of values. The *Meditations* would be the practice of the very theories that it sought to expound as it renewed and increased the receptivity of the Spanish mind, the author's own circumstance, dulled by a feeling of inferiority in the face of what it did not understand.

By meditating on the smallest, nearest things, man becomes most aware first of that which surrounds him and through which he communicates with the universe. Ortega's concept of "circumstance," while indebted to Husserl and William James, was especially suggested by the thought of the Estonian biologist Jakob Johann von Uexküll. It was a concept that had been developing in Ortega's writing since at least as early as 1910.[21] He believed that it helped surpass nineteenth-century ideas of individualism, which he saw as essentially political, by seeing that any individual life is inseparable from its circumstance, from which it derives its potential, and to which it gives new meaning. It is both our destiny and our raw material as we imbue it with our own vision, based on understanding and appreciation. There is no other route to what lies beyond us; hence, "I am I and my circumstance, and if I do not save it, I do not save myself" (I, 322). This total life is part of a greater fabric, a system of relationships.

Rather than an absolute of interpretation, then, it was essential to recognize as many perspectives as there are viewers, and that each of these perspectives is an integral component of reality. Reality as seen by God is the sum of this infinity of viewpoints and to impose one is to assume God's role. Our perspective permits us, by starting with the small and the near, to appreciate superior and sublime values and put our life in its proper relationship to them. Thus we "reabsorb" our circumstance by placing it within the context of a system of relationships, bound together by an estimative hierarchy. Let us understand the hidden sense of all that surrounds us, everything that limits and thereby defines our life, without scorn for even the smallest realities. Only in this way can we pass from the immediate and spontaneous to culture, which is the refined, timeless product, the ideal abstraction of individual, spontaneous lives. Ortega intended here to look at Quixotism as a part of Cervantes's life, as a response to his circumstance and as a telling clue to the "species" Cervantes. The aim was to halt the consideration of Quixotism torn out of its context of vital relationships. Don Quixote was the point at which all Spaniards came together and therein lay the key to their collective destiny: "now we must find a new Spain" (I, 328), with the old one as guide.

In the "Preliminary Meditation," Ortega's splendid literary gifts took flight as he wrote from El Escorial, using its forest as his image for latency, the quality of something to remain ever hidden, to be precisely what cannot be seen, and to exist for us insofar as it creates in us the impression of always being just another step away. Latent reality requires actions of us as it makes us aware of what is capable of yet being discovered, and Ortega used this as a demonstration of the multiplicity of destinies which we must understand and appreciate. Depth and surface must be understood as different, but interdependent and inseparable. A merely passive vision reveals only patent reality, but latency requires looking, an intellectual effort. The patent world is life, executant, and demands nothing of me, but there is a further world that cannot exist without my consciousness of it. It is the realm of conceptual realities like "science, art, justice, courtesy, and religion" (I, 336); in short, culture, the result of man's coming to grips with his circumstance. Seeing gives us only the chaos of primary reality, while looking is concepts and ideas. Thus, each surface is a sort of foreshortening (*escorzo*): it both shows and suggests as things are related in a context which, in turn, is part of a point of view. The more relationships that are established for a thing, the greater its reality.

In the Spain of the Restoration, the low esteem in which *Don Quixote* was held was indicative of a period that lacked a sense of values. The closed, exclusive minds were prevented from looking at the depths of the book, for "just as there is a seeing that is a looking, so is there a reading that is *intellegere*, or reading within. Only thus does *Don Quixote* give up its deep meaning" (I, 340). Latency is the magic of the book, a fact better recognized abroad. In one arc, Ortega embraced philosophical technique, literary appreciation, and social reform. Spain needed the influence of the conceptual ability that was so highly developed in Germanic culture in order to balance the sensuality of Mediterranean culture, more concerned with appearances and impressions than with the thing itself or with concepts and abstract ideals. Spain was still too exclusively limited to sense intuition, and it is only by means of the concept, "the normal organ of profundity" (I, 349), that patent reality is organized into a structure that makes it possible to place each element at the center of a system of relationships so that both its depth and its meaning can be grasped. Concepts are limits that serve both to bring things together and keep them separate in mutual respect, for "if the impression of a thing gives us its material presence, the concept contains everything that this thing is in relation to other things" (I, 351).

Since the concept is a means of completing patent reality, Ortega insisted that no opposition should be established between one and the other, between life and reason. Reason is as much a vital function as the other senses. However, as Marías has shown,[22] Ortega had to

overcome the current dichotomy between rationalism and irrationalism that had one of its finest hours in Unamuno's *Del
sentimiento trágico de la vida* [The Tragic Sense of Life, 1913] and link
reason inextricably with life. Reason is unavoidable in life as man tries
to know what to expect from his circumstance. In the face of the
fleeting quality of the immediate impression, the concept ties things
together in a coherent structure from which further judgments may
be made. Nevertheless, Ortega issued a word of warning: "Be careful, though: not everything is thought, but without it we possess
nothing fully" (I, 354). Life is both surface and depth. The lack of
progression in Spanish culture, Ortega maintained, was due to a lack
of concepts, the firm basis from which man may possess the things in
his circumstance: each artist in the Spanish pantheon is a new Adam,
forced constantly to recreate the world that ceases with him. Each
work lacks a context by which it may be interpreted and while this
gives a rough, basic quality to Spanish culture, the lack of continuity
is debilitating. For a true domination of life, culture is the organizing
instrument, the light that lies within life and is drawn out and cast
back upon it: "Every new concept is a new organ for a previously
invisible part of the world" (I, 358). Only the *Quixote* was an example
of brilliant impressions and surfaces that had an underlying solidity of
conceptual depth.

The "First Meditation" is defined in its subtitle: "Brief Treatise on
the Novel," and it is here that Ortega moved toward the book itself.
Aware that the interest felt by the contemporary reader was due to
what *Don Quixote* has in common with the nineteenth-century novel
that was his circumstance, Ortega set out to define the genre, insist-
ing on the inseparability of form and content as the organ and function. He dismissed the opinion that the novel derives from the epic,
for he saw them as artistic opposites. The epic deals with the past as
absolutely past, an ideal and universalized past that was as archaic to
the first readers as it is to us. In Greek literature in general myths
were the only material considered poetic and the poet enchanted by
means of his skill at telling the themes that his public already knew:
the originality and inventiveness existed before he began his work.
The last offspring of the myths are the books of chivalry, which are
also rooted in an absolute past, and which lack only a belief in that
past. Like the epics, they narrate rather than describe, and their
theme is adventure, to which tension is given by the ever-present
demands of reality. This was the circumstance within which Cervantes worked.

The great advance of Cervantes's art was to bring present reality into literary art. Adventures ceased to be of primary importance and a constant tension was established between poetic and nonpoetic material. It is Sancho's role to represent the intrinsically nonpoetic, in contrast to the poetry of the purely imaginary, and it is in the "frontier nature" of Don Quixote that the two worlds come together. Ortega demonstrated that, since Don Quixote and his will to have adventures are undeniably real, and that the adventures in books of chivalry are undeniably real for him, so adventure and reality become interdependent and each is given greater poetic power by the other. *Don Quixote* is thus very much a product of its time, when psychology began to reveal "the breadth of the inner world, the consciousness, the subjective" (I, 383). Appropriately, "the reality of the adventures is saved, but this is all the more ironical since it is reduced to the psychological so that its reality is that of the material" (I, 384). There are two ways to live such a phenomenon: naively, as is the case of the epic and the books of chivalry; or ironically, as required by the realistic novel, which consciously employs illusions. This latter makes daily reality poetic by converting it into a force that attacks and destroys myth. Naked reality, then, does not become artistic material; merely the process that occurs when it reabsorbs the ideal. Only with a combat between primary and interpreted reality, as so often occurs in *Don Quixote*, does the real become artistically interesting. The purpose of realism is to imitate and to mock; without this comic intention, it lacks aesthetic interest. Consequently, "criticism and jest are not inessential ornaments of *Don Quixote,* but the very texture of the genre, perhaps of all realism" (I, 389).

Cervantes also gave a new dimension to the hero. In the epic, there is harmony because the hero and his desires belong to the same order of possibilities. In *Don Quixote*, however, while the desire is certainly real, the possibility of its successful fulfillment is not. The novel, then, becomes the genre for the hero who, always dissatisfied with an aspect of reality, employs his will either to alter it or dissociate himself from it. By placing Don Quixote precariously on the frontier between patent and latent reality, matter and interpretation, Cervantes gave this struggle special pathos. This meant that the reader could approach heroism either directly, in the belief that it is meaningful and, while painful, capable of conquering reality, thus leading to tragedy; or obliquely, as reality is strengthened sufficiently to crush the heroic effort, provoking comedy. This double possibility is present throughout *Don Quixote*. The hero wills and makes possible his defeat; he is tragic insofar as he wishes to be and insofar as he refuses to renounce the part that he created for himself in his imagination.

Since tragedy occupies a level above us, the reader must have some predisposition to great actions which opens him to things of greater dignity and nobility. Yet just as fantasy is surrounded by reality, so the heroic impulse is constantly besieged by our baser impulses which move us to despise the hero's ambition. We sense in him a force that will break our comfortable inertia and we attack him with the comic and real rather than recognize that he, too, is an example of foreshortening: his patent aspect is visible to all and easily ridiculed, while his latent aspect is a future glory that he alone can perceive. Thus, comedy lives off tragedy in an attempt to preserve an existing situation, and this is the strength of *Don Quixote*. The tragic limit is reached by Don Quixote the hero, and the comic limit by Don Quixote the madman in a book that Ortega classified as a "tragicomedy," a blend that characterizes all novels, but when comic does not necessarily mean humorous. Every novel carries *Don Quixote* within and must provide an ironic criticism of the imaginary. In general, however, Ortega believed that the nineteenth-century novel would not live because the distance between the ideals that it attacks and the reality that is its weapon is so small that there is a lack of poetic dynamism. Reality itself had become so idealized that no other ideal was tolerated. Man was stripped of liberty and so dominated by his material surroundings that they became the only true protagonist. Determinism and a false and misguided dedication to verisimilitude denied tragedy its own truth.

The *Meditations* is an ambiguous work that has been interpreted from contradictory points of view. Ortega commented that "in it one was going to see what was the reaction of my spontaneity to what I had received in Germany, which was, essentially, neo-Kantianism, idealism" (VIII, 43; 1934), yet others see it as a direct result of Ortega's readings in phenomenology.[23] Whereas it is indisputable proof of the serious cast of Ortega's mind and a culmination of his youthful preoccupation with the Spanish circumstance and its need for examples, the fact that it was only an introduction and that Ortega never cast any further light on what he planned to add suggests that some of the ambiguity lay in the mind of the author. It did at least show that Ortega was now more free of his earlier dogmatism and that, as Morón Arroyo has said, "theory, vocation and circumstance reach a perfect balance.[24]

CHAPTER 3

Perspectivism and Biologism

T he nine years following the publication of the *Meditations on Quixote* were a period when Ortega's maturity brought about a growing density in his thought, a concentration of concern and an equilibrium of expression. Moreover, it was the period of four of his greatest publishing ventures: *España* (1915), *El Espectador* (1916), *El Sol* (1917), and the "Biblioteca de Ideas del Siglo XX" (1922). He published almost exclusively articles, yet his personal presence in the life of Spanish letters became pivotal. With characteristic intellectual discipline, he also extended his philosophical depth, at times drawing on lessons offered by current events and at times drawing on that reserved corner of himself that he always retained for freer, more speculative work. The most stunning example of this is *El Espectador* [The Spectator], a private magazine published at irregular intervals until 1934, and containing the most diverse topics.

I   *The Political Circumstance*

While Ortega's work in these years may, for the sake of conveni-ence, be roughly divided into political or social writings, and philosophical works, their interdependence belies any meaningful distinction. The preparation for each major work can be found throughout the lesser writings, for no single work was the result of blinding inspiration, but of laborious elaboration. An astute witness of the country's ambiguous neutrality in World War I, the military rebellion and general strike of 1917, and the formation of the League of Nations, Ortega examined their relationship to the development of Spain in particular and the structure of society in general. Two of his best-known books were the result: *España invertebrada* [Inverte-brate Spain] and *El tema de nuestro tiempo* [The Modern Theme].

A people or a race, he wrote, is held together by a structure of common beliefs, desires, aims, and usages; a common awareness and sense of purpose that maintains a spirit of solidarity or even a spirit of struggle aimed at the molding of a common future. In order to retain cohesiveness, a people must share an ideal that pushes it on to achievement. The tissue of such ideals gives enthusiasm to a society, but when such principles are false, "they are lost, and when they are lost, the nation becomes disjointed, atomized, and the first strong wind that comes along makes it disappear" (X, 272–73; 1915). This shared feeling and common belief must be effectively integrated into the politics of the nation so that it may have the boldness to dare and not paralyze itself with the fear of failure, as was then the case of Spain: "what distinguishes ours from the other countries of Europe is not the number of things that fail in it, but the number of things that are not attempted in it" (X, 278; 1915). For Ortega, the objective recognition of his country's faults was an integral function of his patriotism, a much debated catchword at the time. It was clear that without an increase in her "vital energy" Spain could not move into the new age that Ortega foresaw, and to the clarification of this problem he devoted dozens of articles: "We have spent thirty years looking for what is missing in Spanish life, without really finding it. And the fact is that perhaps what we are missing is precisely life" (II, 524; 1922). Spaniards suffered from "vital anemia," a lack of interest in and enthusiasm for every type of human activity, in public and private life. Spanish life proceeded by means of nervous tics and routine gestures. However, where Angel Ganivet had detected a lack of will in Spain, Ortega saw the will as the one thing that Spain had in abundance, but unfocused, raw and undirected: "we have wanted wanting without ever wanting any thing. In history we are a burst of blind, diffuse, brutal will" (II, 557; 1915). This, coupled with courage, had given Spain both her historical might and her decline.

Since her virtues lacked the underpinnings of a strong social sense, Ortega found Spain socially reactionary, delighting in the absolutely old and unbudgingly intolerant of the new. Moreover, it was a country with no sense of liberty and more willing to find reasons for quarreling than for common enthusiasm. The lack of individual confidence had led to a moral sickness that replaced respect and understanding with rancor and resentment. While it was true, he believed, that Spaniards had advanced greatly since the turn of the century, as a nation they were still inchoate, too ready to accept vulgar standards and unable to discern opportunities for heroic action. Spain had become a mere shadow of her historic mission, marking time in the routine repetition of a dead past: "They were ideas; today they are ruins of ideas" (II, 173; 1916). Lacking a proper vision of the role of individual personality, Spaniards had all too often taken refuge in false traditionalism and an exaggerated belief in the value of Spanish purity (*casticismo*). Ortega considered this to be the worst form of provincialism because it showed that Spaniards were unable to see that a strong personality was sufficient; rather, the Spanish personality consisted in being aggressively demonstrated. The meanness of the Spanish temperament considered even the enjoyment of life as proof of weakness and a lack of manliness.

The inability to evaluate and establish standards was rooted in the Spaniard's "suspicion that to give in to spiritual contagion is the basest thing that a man can do, for it means giving up being a person, being a creator and protagonist of one's own judgments or acts and becoming material pushed and stamped by someone else's influence" (X, 601; 1919). A nation unable to think for itself and weigh viewpoints could not create. Since the country had no notion of what was better or worse, all levels of national life were riddled with an inversion of values that stimulated the triumph of inferiority. To be outstanding was to be scorned, and as a result, it was considered acceptable that culture should become democratic to the point where there should be no scale of values in man's reaction to his circumstance: "All the shortcomings and defects of Spanish life will be incorrigible as long as we are happy confusing the able with the inept, the noble with the base" (II, 131; 1917).

Since those who made up the great mass lacked an individual sense of themselves, the need for a minority capable of making distinctions and undertaking the thoughtful tasks had become inescapable. Whereas the average man simply coincides with his surroundings by thinking as everyone else does, the lot of the superior man is one of inherent tragedy, always in the vanguard and resigned to being the object of misunderstanding, envy, and scorn. The immediate fact was that such a role was not being filled in Spain by any group. Although such a reform was moral and social, there could be no denying that politicians, by dint of their visibility, could in some measure set the tone for national standards. Ortega sadly concluded that in the main the politicians of Spain offered the poorest example for their people, and that it was unreasonable to expect of them even a minimal amount of courtesy, dignity or respect for the opinions of others.

Even individual liberty was threatened. The lack of solidarity blinded people to the fact that any reduction of one person's or one group's freedom reduced that of everyone, and Ortega was repeatedly obliged to conclude: "We can place little trust in the liberal sensitivity of our country. No one or almost no one has that thin skin that makes an individual in other races feel the wounds that he receives in his civic honor and in his fundamental rights" (X, 662; 1920). He was scrupulous, however, about distinguishing between a superstitious faith in democracy as an absolute value, an attitude left over from an earlier time, and the concept of true liberalism. In 1917, he insisted that "he who is irritated at seeing equals treated unequally but is not disturbed by seeing people who are not equal treated equally, is not democratic, he is plebeian" (II, 138). Absolute democracy is preposterous, for society should aim at the equalization not of rights, but of privileges (*privus + legis*). When restricted to politics, democracy seems unsurpassable, "but exasperated and uncontrolled democracy, democracy in religion or art, democracy in thought and gesture, democracy in the heart and in habits is the most dangerous disease from which a society can suffer" (II, 135; 1917). Absolute democracy provokes a disintegration of the structure that gives society its dynamism.

As he had done in "Old and New Politics," he attributed many of the social maladies of Spain to the breakdown of healthy structures capable of serving as links between social extremes. Not only was the state incapable of exerting the influence necessary to bring Spaniards into the life of their country, but it was guilty of contributing to the disintegration with actions that virtually set citizens at each other's throats. Still, this was tacitly supported by "the great crowd of 'neutral' Spaniards, with the worst of 'neutralities,' which is that of inaction, of laziness or of a senseless cowardice mixed with grotesque frivolity" (X, 522; 1919). Politicians were merely citizens with louder voices and exaggerated gestures, bereft of vision, and the press, which commanded enormous power, served only to publicize their actions. It was natural that most Spaniards felt disenfranchised and ignored and perpetuated the characteristic national attitudes of disrespect and pessimism.

The state had to reestablish itself as an all-inclusive structure, giving cohesiveness to its diverse elements, providing them with a hope of success. Without such a structure, Spain would continue to be "invertebrate" (XI, 266; 1917) and unduly susceptible to revolution. Spanish governments had all too often shown themselves ready to use repression as a weapon to remove the possibility of revolution, but the invocation of the law or abstract principles of order by the state could not justify the violence exercised by the authorities to

control the diverse forces within society, for "the injustice of authority inevitably engenders social illegality" (X, 526; 1919). Respect for
rights must be first, and justice then recognizes them, but justice is
necessarily relative and subsequent to those rights. The life of the
nation and its people must be the determining factor, the origin and
goal of all national action: "Proclaim the supremacy of vital power—
work, knowledge and enjoyment—over any other power. Let us
learn to expect everything from ourselves and to fear everything from
the state. In short, national politics rather than state politics" (X, 280;
1915).

He repeatedly called for new, untried men in the highest offices.
While aware that they might prove no better than those whom they
replaced, he believed that they would, at the very least, be unmarked
by previous disgrace and could enjoy some degree of public confidence. He continued to be concerned by the division of political
parties into Liberal and Conservative, for it was still more false since
the First World War, when politics abroad had come to rely on subtler
shadings. Nonetheless, the two great Spanish parties, both essentially of the Right, continued to share power because they shared the
confidence of the king. Alfonso XIII maintained his preference for
weak men who would please him, rather than for decisive leaders
capable of serving the needs of the nation. As a result, a man's
standing in the eyes of the king seemed to be in inverse relation to his
real political value. The king tended to favor the Conservatives,
thereby forcing the true Left into ever more radical stances as they
saw all their more progressive attitudes stolen from them and turned
over to Rightist governments by the Crown.

Ortega believed that the greatest danger lay in the division of
power between the Crown and Parliament that had been established
by the Constitution of 1876. The king had so weakened Parliament
that, as the masses moved inexorably to the Left, the Crown would
ultimately find itself faced with the rising new social forces from
which it was by nature so removed and which it could therefore not
hope to understand or control. Such an antihistorical system represented the immediate interests of only the oligarchy and the
monarchy. The monarchy had succeeded in increasing its power, but
only by usurping that of other levels of society, and by 1922 Ortega
could openly complain that "the place where the politicians plot most
is the palace" (XI, 22). The morally correct path would be to cease
tinkering with the governmental process and intervene only in
specific, constitutional instances and in favor of responsible govern-

ments. Ortega was not yet critical of the monarchy as an institution for, contrary to what was often said, he believed that Europe was moving toward new forms of monarchy. In this, he was mistaken.

II *The Lessons of the War*

Spain remained officially neutral throughout the First World War, although the king in fact extended important technical courtesies to Germany. Throughout the Continent, many writers chose sides and devoted themselves to their causes, but this role deeply troubled Ortega, who maintained silence for about a year. The division of European intellectuals into bands struck him as contrary to their true calling, and he attributed it to passion, rather than to reason. Yet from 1915 onward he, too, remarked frequently on the significance of the conflict, while attempting to limit his partisan comments. He believed that there was a further lesson to be drawn.

He believed the war to be the result of a neo-Romantic enthusiasm for nationalism that had become increasingly evident since about 1900. Germany had been late in reaching the forefront of history, only to discover that the world had already been divided among the great powers, thereby preventing her from fulfilling the destiny that she felt to be hers. Ortega believed that she had undertaken the war because of an irresistible need to expand. He accepted neither the view that the war indicated the failure of civilization or of its most enduring values nor the idea that the conflict had grown out of a cultural divergence. Rather, he saw it as a fight between Germans and Slavs on the one hand and between German economic interests and those of France and England on the other. However, while he did not consider Germany to be antidemocratic, he did dislike her imperialistic tendencies and her state-oriented concept of democracy. Fully aware that the victor in the war would necessarily have a deep influence on Spain as well as on the vanquished nations, he declared himself in favor of the triumph of England, although not with great enthusiasm.

Ortega was never a true pacifist, for he believed that, in many ways, like revolution within a country, the possibility of war had to exist always. While he despised all its horrors and violence, he recognized that war has an invigorating effect on the human spirit and brings with it new attempts at reform. In 1916, in "The Genius of War," a response to Max Scheler's book, he stated that war clarifies and puts into perspective human attitudes, and went on to respond to

Scheler by stating that "there are, in fact, in war a biological motor and a spiritual impulse that are high values for humanity. The desire to rule, the will that the superior organize and govern the inferior, constitute two sovereign ethical impulses. But if in war *there is* this, war *is not* this" (II, 204; 1916). The difficulty lay in distinguishing between moral (just) and immoral (unjust) wars, a distinction that rested on a superior concept of justice to which international law had not yet successfully addressed itself. The mere question of strength could not, as Scheler claimed, be used as proof of superiority, nor could the exercise of force by a state be interpreted in terms of civil law, as if the state were an individual. Humanitarian passivism, he reasoned, effectively espoused inertia as a social goal, failing to recognize that important distinctions had to be made. Moreover, war as an impulse was the struggle for power, which included the struggle of something new to displace something old. Despite such ethical considerations, World War I seemed "sad, monotonous and morally deaf"(II, 29; 1916) to Ortega, who chafed somewhat under Spain's neutrality.[1].

The Armistice of 1918 and the Paris Peace Conference of 1919 had as their consequence two effects that were of great interest to Ortega. First, Europe had decisively moved to the Left, a shift that could only make more risky the political situation in Spain. Second, of great symbolic impact, was the call for the formation of the League of Nations. To some extent, he saw it as an international enterprise that could unite countries "in search of the ideals of human liberty and just democracy" (X, 503; 1919), to which it was essential that Spain subscribe. It would give all countries the opportunity to participate in world affairs, while emphasizing their responsibility to make themselves worthy of the founding principles. It was the institution for the new period that was beginning, and Ortega called for participation from all levels of Spanish life in a new social movement that would transcend political parties and exclude only "the men who have governed this Spain that we are trying to bury" (X, 462; 1918).

Within Spain's boundaries, the working class and the army had begun to exert an increasing influence on the development of the country. Ortega welcomed the rise of the proletariat, for it was the only class that seemed to have a clear, although frequently misguided, sense of its own potential. Moreover, the workers represented a resistance to the essential conservatism of the traditional parties that appeared to believe that any compromise with the workers would represent a debasement of public power. Ortega held that intellectuals had more in common with the workers than with the national oligarchy, and he acted to establish a common ground upon which all these forces could come together (X, 453, 455, 478; 1918). Nevertheless, both workers and the Socialist movement seemed unwilling to see the threats to their cause. One of the most dramatic was the series of assassinations carried out in Barcelona in 1920 which, while not the fault of responsible workers' socialism, did cast a shadow over their movement in the eyes of those who opposed their rise. The relative indifference shown by the workers' groups to "this bloodying of the Socialist idea" (X, 675; 1920) caused Ortega deep concern. Likewise, he urged them to move away from the abstract utopianism of the international union of workers, which he felt had lost credibility during the war, and from the dogmas of Marx and Sorel, which he found specious and unrealistic in that they deluded workers into believing that direct action was a worthy course. There was a lack of subtlety in the movement that led to perversions of the liberal spirit which should be vigorously resisted if the workers were not to become as fanatical and narrowminded as the ruling classes.

The other important group that was being deprived of its due place in the Spanish social structure was the army, which had been allowed to become dangerously demoralized. Spain's controversial intervention in Morocco had provoked widespread public hostility, and the country's neutrality in World War I had left the army feeling removed from the rest of the nation and largely despised by it. In November 1916 members of the Infantry formed Committees of Defense (*Juntas de Defensa*) in Barcelona with a view to eliminating favoritism in promotions, achieving adequate payment for the military in the face of the rising cost of living, and more significantly, to resist the capricious influence of the office in the royal palace that saw that the king's wishes were carried out. The Committees reflected the growing influence of syndicalism in Catalonia and their stated goals were perfectly consonant with the mood of the country. However, they soon overstepped acceptable limits and the inevitable crisis was reached in May 1917, when the government ordered the imprisonment of the Committees' leaders. By this time, the Committees had achieved such power and the government had lost so much authority that the Cabinet was forced to resign. In June 1917, in "Bajo el arco en ruina" [Beneath the Ruined Arch], the article that was to provoke his separation from *El Imparcial*, Ortega perceptively analyzed the Committees' significance for the future of the country: "a week ago, the form of government changed in Spain. The effective power lies in the Committees of Defense of the Infantry" (XI, 266; 1917). The army had placed itself beyond the law, yet enjoyed the support of the people. While Ortega, like most of the Left, sympathized with its goals, the example was dangerous and the situation was in fact "more serious than a revolution" (ibid.), for the army's step not only violated the Constitution, but annulled it. Noting with some satisfaction that "since the first of June Spaniards seem to prefer vital Spain to official Spain" (X, 357; 1917), he joined the demand for a Constituent Parliament that would create a new political structure.[2]

However, 1917 was to become one of the benchmarks of social upheaval as the conflicts between government and the nation grew. In August the country was paralyzed by the general strike that, on the one hand, represented an attempt by the labor movement to take advantage of the mood for reform that had been brought to the surface by the military, but on the other hand, was in large part put down by the army. Ortega attributed the harshness of the army's actions in part to its desire to show that, despite the illegality of its own rebellion in June, it was still the force of order in the country. The violent suppression of the strike was a generally popular move, and both labor and the army were eventually outmaneuvered by the king and the cabinet. In 1918, Ortega assessed the overall results of the Committees and the strike: "In my judgment, the cause of the two failures is the same, and moreover, is extremely simple. The Committees of Defense were popular as long as it appeared that they wanted to transform the nation while taking the nation into account, that is to say, other Spaniards who are not soldiers. The strike in August was unpopular because it aspired also to reform the rest of us Spaniards who are not workers, or republicans, or reformists, without in any way taking us into account" (X, 426; 1918). The Committees of Defense had overstepped the limits of public support by becoming too sure of their power and nearly constituting a parallel government that would have usurped the rights of both the monarchy and the Parliament. Nonetheless, Ortega saw that a death blow had been dealt to the old system and that renewal could be at hand.

The unrest had shown that a thorough redistribution of wealth was both feasible and essential if social chaos was to be avoided: "It is necessary to achieve with all possible haste a social state in which no one fails to earn a certain minimum and no one earns more than what a work is worth" (X, 588; 1919). This required that serious policies be enacted to give muscle to a social structure in which the people's idea of what their institutions should be corresponded to what they in fact were. The means of renewal were still liberalism, socialism, and democracy: "To economic justice, by means of improved democracy, perfected in its instruments!" (X, 590; 1919). Socialism was not to be like the results of the Soviet revolution of 1917 that had momentarily captured the imagination of so many men of the Left, but far more liberal and thus, individual. While the war had demonstrated the inadequacy of nineteenth-century social theories, Ortega was careful to point out that this in no way proved the error of the underlying social laws that those theories attempted to describe. Rather, the theories had to be revised and revitalized to correspond to the new realities brought to the surface by the war. In 1918, he described the reforms needed in Spain, including freedom of conscience, a secular state, constitutional protection of freedoms, the abolition of the Senate, a greater voice for the working class and the creation of a new ministry that would enact a program to educate the workers so that they could become more effectively organized in order to take greater control of their own affairs (X, 469–71; 1918). The idea that he was to pursue most vigorously, however, was the decentralization of the state.

Since his youth he had believed that "the realization of Spanish life" could best be achieved by means of a concrete policy that would "correct Madrid with the provincial capitals, and the provincial capitals with the villages" (II, 262; 1915). To give the country a truly inclusive structure, it was necessary that select minorities be developed in every district in order to overcome the alienation and resultant resentment felt by so many Spaniards: "Instead of a single head, as enormous as it is vague, let us rather stir in the body of Spain, which is today without a structure, a multitude of lesser, but energetic and competent, heads" (VI, 218; 1917). Unfortunately, the question of increased regional autonomies was too readily reduced to the "Catalonian question," which was one of the complaints of the Committees of Defense and which Ortega believed to be merely the pull of the strongest region away from the unity of a weak country.[3] It was the antithesis of the goal to which he aspired, for he believed that regional autonomy, by strengthening the sense of purpose of individual regions, would increase, rather than diminish, the solidarity of the nation. In other countries, the war had succeeded in bringing about the reform or even the elimination of outdated institutions and had shaken countries out of their inertia. The events of 1917, Ortega hoped, would achieve similar results in Spain and for several years he was to become ever more convinced that a military government might be not merely necessary, but desirable. In 1920, faced with the almost total ineptitude of Parliament, he declared that "the moment has come for the military to advance to the government. Now that they exercise power, let them have the responsibility for it" (X, 626). No other force seemed capable of effecting deep change in the country; Parliament and civil authority clearly represented a mere constitutional fiction.

III   España invertebrada

Ortega seems to have been somewhat surprised by the popular success of *España invertebrada,* but the fact remains that it was the right book at the right time. The nine chapters of the first part were published in *El Sol* between December 1920 and May 1921, when they were collected in book form. By October of that same year, however, a second edition was necessary and it is in the prologue to this edition that Ortega conveyed concern that his schematically expressed ideas might be misread by a broader public than the one for whom he claimed to have been writing. In 1922, a third edition appeared that included a second part, consisting of seven more articles published in *El Sol* since February of that year.

Spain still staggered under the weight of her excessively idealized past, at the expense of a clear vision of her present and the future. In consequence, the aim of Ortega's articles was a critical reinterpretation of the structure of her history. Influenced to some degree by Spengler's *Decline of the West* (1918), he recognized that, like the other major European nations, Spain was passing through a crucial historical moment that had begun before World War I, which was merely a symptom. Given the lack of national purposes and ideals throughout the Continent, it was possible that Spain already held the key to her own regeneration if she could only develop the skills to use it. Such was his aim. The first of the two principal sections of the book, "Particularism and Direct Action," sets forth an analysis of the forces of association and dissociation that characterize the life of any national unit. Ortega rejected the common belief that a nation is the result of the expansion of an initial nucleus in which the characteristics of other units disappear through assimilation. Rather, he believed that a nation is born as preexisting social units are joined into a larger structure, motivated by a suggestive project of a life in common, some undertaking that can be achieved only through a union of strengths. The dynamism of the national unit is the result of the ever-present centrifugal force exerted by all the smaller units in contrast to the centripetal character of the nucleus. The nucleus, however, possesses a *quid divinum*, an unpredictable quality of being able to conceive of great enterprises and of knowing how to lead all sectors toward their fulfillment.

The integration of Spain had been possible because Castile, from the beginning, revealed this centripetal impulse. Through her centuries-long struggle against the Moors, she became aware of her affinity with the rest of the Peninsula and conceived the idea of a unified Spain. With the marriage of Ferdinand and Isabella came the first true *Weltpolitik* through the joining of Aragón, whose politics traditionally looked to Europe; and Castile, whose politics was turned toward Africa. The national project was to spread the energy of Spain throughout the world, and as long as such projects endured, Spain remained intact. The disintegration and decay began in the colonies in 1580, where it spread until the loss of the last overseas colonies brought the disintegration inside the Peninsula. Within the country, it became "particularism," that stage in the life of a nation when each group ceases to feel that it is a part of the whole and senses that, since there is no common ideal or goal, it no longer has a role to play. Paradoxically, particularism originates in the center of society's power structure. Since the time of Philip III, Castile had taken on no new projects, preferring to maintain the status quo in a bitter and narrow spirit. The Church and the monarchy identified their own destinies with that of the nation and, by a process of "inverse selection" (III, 70), the best men ceased to be chosen for the most important tasks.

When particularism becomes a national characteristic, social groups no longer see themselves as interdependent and "social elasticity" (III, 74) is lost. With the dissipation of this feeling that each life is reflected in and multiplied by all others, a nation becomes polarized and ceases to be a society. Direct action is the inevitable outcome, for to those who feel cut off recourse to public institutions such as Parliament and the courts seems to be a humiliating capitulation to enemies whom they do not respect and whose very right to exist in the same national entity they deny. Such action reveals a belief that it is not necessary to reason or even to fight in order to impose views, because of the conviction that they are shared by everyone: "Direct action, in short, is the tactic of the winner, not of the fighter" (III, 83). This desire to conquer without effort was symptomatic of a social irresponsibility that excluded and separated, and that requires no *quid divinum* at all.

In the second part, "The Absence of Betters," Ortega undertook the first systematic development of his "aristocratic" theory of society. Here, however, his concern was specifically with a Spain that was deluding herself with the idea that her current situation was due to a lack of strong leadership. Ortega sensed rather that the people were in fact no longer willing to believe in the abilities of leaders in any field. Since he saw great men as the depositaries of a collective mythology in whom the people wish to believe and therefore to follow, he considered the creation of leaders to be one of the responsibilities of the masses.

History displays an alternation between periods in which societies and aristocracies are formed with vigor, and periods of disintegration, such as that at the end of which Spain then found herself. When a nation is in its historically ascendant period, the mass senses its role and is able to feel enthusiasm for those people whom it considers superior. In a period of decay and particularism, however, the mass becomes the standard and rejects all signs of excellence, thereby refusing to fulfill its social function. Limited to politics, such a phenomenon would affect only the surface of national life, but when it infects "the socializing activity" (III, 94) of a country, the disintegration becomes characteristic of all aspects of human activity. Eventually, however, the masses would be faced with their own inadequacy: "Beyond petulance they will discover in themselves a new spiritual state: resignation, which in most men is the only fertile soil and the highest form of spirituality that they can reach. Upon it will it be possible to begin the new construction" (III, 44). Once the mass has experienced its own failure, it will be ready again to see the need to be led by its betters.

Ortega did not distinguish between mass and elite on the basis of blood or class, but on the basis of an individual's ability to fulfill his social destiny: "in every class, in every group that does not suffer serious anomalies, there always exist a vulgar mass and an oustanding minority" (III, 103). This minority, in a properly functioning society, is such that others feel a natural impulse to follow and even emulate its example. Ortega called this "docility," the basis for an "aristocracy," in the sense where *aristos* means "best." It is the attraction of the many by the few, but when the minority loses its qualities of excellence and ceases to set standards, it is the duty of the mass to discern this and establish a new minority. If, however, the mass rebels merely in order to establish itself as the standard to be achieved, it eliminates the possibility of a true aristocracy because it no longer believes it necessary and may, in fact, consider it repressive. This lack of a scale of values is at the root of the spirit of particularism and social chaos.

The history of Spain is marked by the dearth of models who have left an individual imprint, with the result that "here the 'people' have done everything, and what the 'people' could not do has remained undone" (III, 109). Ortega saw the colonization (but not the conquest) of America as Spain's only truly great accomplishment, but pointed out that even it was an achievement of the people, with the result that the defects of the colonies were precisely those of the colonizers: a certain lack of discipline, of a lively culture, and of a progressive civilization. In France and England, however, we see a history created by minorities, despite a specific historical structure identical to that of Spain: a relatively homogeneous autocthonous race, the sediment of Roman civilization, and a Germanic invasion. Discarding as not decisive the Arab presence in Spain, Ortega found the differentiating factor to have been the race of the Germanic invaders. Spain was invaded by the Visigoths, the most civilized and least energetic Germanic race, which readily accepted Roman civilization at the expense of the development of its own, the most characteristic form of which, if we are to judge by the example of the Franks, would have been feudalism, in which the only State was "a series of personal and private relationships between lords" (III, 116). In short, a ruling minority. Although in France this minority was very powerful, it scarcely existed among the Visigoths and they were easily swept from the Peninsula by the Moors. As a result, Spain's moment of glory (1480–1600) was due to chance, for she could be unified precisely because of the weakness of her pluralism and the lack of forceful personalities who could cause division, while the rest of Europe was still broken up among various feudal or postfeudal leaders. Ortega thus concluded that Spain's entire history, if it had ever been healthy, could be said to have been an endless process of decay.

Nevertheless, he believed that the "Modern Age" was reaching its close and that the gradually waning strength of the greater nations would now leave an opening for the lesser peoples. The historical circumstances were right for Spain to recreate herself. Although he felt that particularism had to be overcome, as well as certain abuses and signs of fanaticism, the root of the problem was to be found in the very soul of the Spanish people which rejects excellence simply because it is excellence and which considers itself to be the final authority for its own political, moral, and artistic governance. Spain must, then, set herself the task of curing this "radical perversion of the social instincts" (III, 125), but first it was necessary to await the crisis, the total failure of the masses, at which time the restoration could be rapid and glorious.

IV   *Biologism and Vitalism*

As Ortega matured as a thinker, the concept of "life," in all its manifestations, came to occupy a large portion of his thought, making sociological, pedagogical, historiographical, and philosophical texts increasingly interdependent. At least as early as 1911 he had begun to concern himself with "the vital" (I, 551). In the first volume of *El Espectador* (1916), he included a fragment from a course offered at the University in 1915–16. Entitled "Conciencia, objeto y las tres distancias de éste" [Consciousness, Object and the Three Distances of the Latter], the essay represents both the influence of and, to a less successful extent, an attempt to surpass, Husserl's phenomenology.

As indicated by the title, he returned to the much-discussed problem of the relationship between consciousness and the realities with which it is concerned. He recognized that while such objects as a rose and a centaur are different in that one is "real" and the other is not, both are nonetheless beings, distinguished by the mode by which they enter and become an object of consciousness, which is the characteristic that they have in common. Since consciousness, perception, and imagination are all dependent upon being in function of an object which is not them, but from which they are inseparable, it is clear that while the rose is a being of perception, the centaur is a being of fantasy. Thus, consciousness, while indivisible, consists of a duality: it is "an attitude or an action of a subject and a something towards which this action is directed," and is therefore "the union of two totally different things: my action of referring to, and that to which I refer" (II, 62–63; 1916). This latter is, of course, the object and is anything to which a subject may refer, whether "real" or not.

However, an object may exist in relation to the subject in any of three modes, or distances. The closest and most obvious is *presence,* being there. This is, said Ortega, a matter of perceptions or *present-ations* and deals with what is called "real." The second distance is a matter of representation or imagining and is the mode of *absence,* as in a picture or a memory. Ortega insisted that this is not a merely negative characteristic, "but a positive being absent and being only represented" (II, 64). He chose the example of the plastic arts which contain, intermixed, these first two modes: one present, which is the materiality of the matter employed; the other absent and referred to: what is depicted in the work as art. These two objects of consciousness, one perceived and the other imagined, have aesthetic value only when united. The third distance, or *reference*, is an understanding (although not necessarily a knowledge) of the object through signs and words. It enables us to deal with things without possessing any knowledge of them nor any scrap of them upon which to base ourselves. Especially irritating to the positivists and sensualists, this mode, Ortega believed, should endow the word "mention" with the dignity of a technical term that embraces that which is omitted from both perception (presence) and representation (absence).

In the published fragments, he did not carry his observations to clearly defined conclusions, but the work reveals that he had already begun to go beyond the *Meditations*. In two other essays that appeared in the same volume of *El Espectador*, "Verdad y perspectiva" [Truth and Perspective], and "Nada 'moderno' y 'muy siglo XX'" [Not at all "Modern" and "Very Twentieth-Century"], which is in some measure its continuation, he explained that the legacy of the late nineteenth century—positivism and utilitarianism—through which the past was still seen, retained too great an influence, particularly in Spain, and that it was time for the younger generation to supersede it. As a correlative of a utilitarian period dominated by political concerns, nineteenth-century culture had too often seen the means as ends, but World War I had given a vivid demonstration, if any were needed, of the failure of such attitudes, and Ortega called for a new perspective that would encourage "useless" (nonutilitarian) thought, which alone could clarify ultimate truths. He did not claim that the theoretic mode was superior, but rather that it was a necessary adjunct to and witness of spontaneous life. Hence the title *El Espectador* for the journal devoted to such concerns.

The new, vitalist perspective would surpass the traditional dichotomy of thought that leads either to the skepticism which believes that only the individual point of view exists and that truth is therefore unattainable, or to rationalism which demands a point of view beyond the individual. It was Ortega's aim to avoid both solutions, declaring: "The individual point of view seems to me the only point of view from which one can look at the world in its truth. Anything else is a trick" (II, 18). Reality is one with the individual perspective; consequently, the individual true to his mission is irreplaceable in that he sees a facet of reality invisible to everyone else, but no less true. Indeed, each perspective implies a different set of values, since what is in the foreground for one may be in the background for another, and the attention devoted to each element will differ. Ortega felt that the new post-Modern age demanded a new sensitivity: instead of a "modern" culture of means and utilitarianism that could not conceive that the dynamics of life could render it outmoded, a "twentieth-century" culture concerned with ultimate questions and that did not confuse usefulness with truth.

It was during this period that Ortega's appreciation of the forms and rhythms of history began to acquire greater subtlety. As early as 1916 he saw that while the study of history must cease being the mere accumulation of data and become a scientific discipline, it could serve only as an adjunct to vitality: "every interpretation is a supplanting, it is never the text itself. The philosophy of history provides a rational interpretation of life, but the vital text remains outside it: the vital text is made up of the expansions and contractions of my heart . . ." (II, 160).

The very existence of his own generation, so different from, while inextricably related to, the one that preceded it (which was in turn, quite unlike, yet descended from, the previous one), was proof that the very character of life changes as each generation brings forth its unique values and perspectives. Ortega was preparing the way for a greater sensitivity to "the modulations of the human melody throughout time" (II, 517; 1922), and was able to affirm that "perhaps the most delicate conquest of the contemporary age, a conquest of which very little advantage has been taken, is the historical sense, by means of which we look out onto past times, and in a way enjoy their pleasures and tremble with their pains" (II, 516). The emotional vocabulary is an integral part of his evolving philosophy of history in that scientific understanding of a period must include an appreciation not merely of what happened, but of how and why it happened, what was the state of mind that provoked an event and that was provoked by it. In order to understand this, it is necessary to understand those forces of man's vitality that historical studies traditionally ignore in favor of factual events: "it is not that life in one period is different from that in another because its ideas, arts, politics, industry, are different, but rather the reverse; two periods have different ideas, arts, politics and industry because the radical feeling of life in them is different" (II, 517). The word "life" must be given its fullest and most tangible meaning here. Each period must be understood as possessing a peculiar "vital pulse" that defines it and to discover and study this is, according to Ortega, one of life's most sublime pleasures.

In a series of articles published in *El Sol* in 1920, Ortega's thought could be seen to have entered definitively on its "biologistic" stage.[4] Somewhat misleadingly entitled "El *Quijote* en la escuela" [The *Quixote* in School], the articles have as one of their concerns the application to psychology and educational theory of the then relatively new (1902) theories of Bayliss and Starling regarding internal secretions.

Heretofore, only two classes of spiritual activity had been considered worthy of inclusion in educational principles: the mechanical or technical activity that is civilization, and the cultural functions that spring from an intimate psychic need but nonetheless conform to certain norms. Ortega, however, defended the equal dignity of spontaneous life, which is at the heart of all individual existence. It makes culture and civilization possible for it alone provides the psychic impulses, such as feelings and thinking, that are previous to other classes of vitality and lead to them. The curiosity that exists spontaneously leads to the search for knowledge that is science and this in turn makes possible the technology of civilization. Therefore, while culture and civilization must be dealt with in higher education, primary education must have as its objective the promotion and enrichment of the spontaneous life that is characteristic of the child. Civilization and culture would alter, but the spontaneous impulses are truly timeless; only their degree of intensity can be improved. The assumption that the child must be led from (*e-ducare*) childhood into a specific medium of maturity is destructive of the child's spontaneous creativity. Rather than impose a less varied maturity upon him, let him instead create his own maturity out of his spontaneous life, the treasure of childhood that artists and other "culminating personalities" manage to preserve: "maturity is not a suppression, but an integration of childhood" (II, 299). The best of man is the child that endures within him, influencing his every act.

In biology, a revolution was taking place that, to Ortega's delight, recognized that "vitality is previous to and the creator of its concrete function" (II, 285). Just as it was now seen that the apparently useless activities of the body such as internal secretions were vital and essential, likewise, he contended, the psyche possesses functions that, despite or because of their apparent uselessness, are closer to life itself than had previously been seen. Of the internal psychic functions, the feelings are the deepest; while seeming to be superfluous, they are in fact the root of all higher creations. Ortega demonstrated this through an examination of wanting and desiring as psychic functions. Whereas the first is directed outward and always

implies an obtainable object, the second refers to a "relatively or
absolutely impossible" object (II, 287). One may desire something
without wanting it because desire is an internal function that stimulates the appetite and thus the will. It has a regulatory function in the
psyche and the greater the number of desires felt, the greater the
need for selection and for the establishment of a hierarchy among
them.

A large capacity for desires springs from spontaneous life and
reflects an abundance of vitality and an enriched taste and capacity for
culture and civilization. This, then, is the proper goal of primary
education: "A pedagogy of internal secretions . . . will try to foster
appetites and create an abundant stock of them in the youthful soul"
(II, 289). Such an education would contribute to the formation of
"vitally perfect" individuals whose psychic health would provide the
atmosphere for noble and generous attitudes. Ortega now saw the
medium as being limited to that which exists "vitally" for the subject.
There is no unique medium to which all must adapt, but rather a
medium for each organism, for each life, or in the case of education,
for each child. What exists vitally for one may be sterile for another
because of a differing sensitivity. However, the richer one's capacity
for feeling, the more objects exist for him: "Not only does the organism adapt to the medium, but the medium adapts to the organism.
. . . The body is only half of the living being: its other half is the
objects that exist for it . . ." (II, 298). Instead of merely adapting the
child to a ready-made environment, the medium would be adapted to
and by the individual. Since a child imbued with strong and varied
feelings would be more confident of himself and of the universe, he
should be reared in a world in which only the desirable, which
increases his eagerness for life, is allowed to exist. Anything that
could have a restraining effect must be banished from the psychic
landscape. The richest life is not that governed by utilitarianism, but
that which creates spontaneously, sportively: "Culture is not the
daughter of work, but of sport" (II, 302), and history has always
moved between these two extremes, alternately favoring one and
then the other.

V   El tema de nuestro tiempo

Published as a book in 1923, but based upon Ortega's university
lectures of 1921–22, *El tema de nuestro tiempo* (inappropriately translated as *The Modern Theme*) was an accentuation of his biologism and

one of the first major expositions of the philosophical posture that would define his ratiovitalism. As he indicated some years later, he had reservations about the book, but he considered the ideas that it contained to be of some importance (VIII, 15; 1934).

Reaffirming his conviction that the movement of generations throughout history represents a system of shifting perspectives that must be met by appropriate philosophical responses, he urged his own generation to surpass ideologies that exerted a hold only because they were already in place. Since Socrates discovered reason, and especially since the Renaissance, the history of thought has been marked by the conflict between rationalism and relativism. Ortega found both too exclusive, for rationalism since the time of Descartes had shown itself to be absolutist, able to accept only the quantitative world and immutable truth, while relativism postulated the truth only of individual convictions. The former was unable to deal with qualitative reality and the forces of life, which nevertheless continued to seem real to man, while the latter was merely skepticism that, by denying all absolute truth, rendered absurd the truth of its own assertions. Man has lived divided between the living changeability of historical reality and the need for a firm basis that permits him to attain a lasting truth. The ideology of Descartes, however, had prevailed with the result that "modern sensibility" had been predicated upon a belief that man is a totally rational being. This "modern" period, Ortega claimed, was drawing to a close; the world had entered an age of transition and man must show himself able to perceive "the other kind of reason that is not pure but vital" (III, 161), and to reject the false dilemma between life and truth.

Ortega conceived of thinking as an organic function that is both a vital necessity and an indispensable instrument for life. It is both subjectively useful and governed by a need and an impulse for objective truth; thus it represents an adjustment between myself and that which is not I: "To be true, thought must coincide with things, with what transcends me; but, at the same time, for this thought to exist, I must think it, I must adhere to its truth, give it an intimate place in my life, make it immanent in the small biological sphere that is myself " (III, 166). Something that is part of me also transcends me and obeys objective laws; these laws are what we call culture, "the repertory of vital functions whose products or results have a consistency beyond life" (III, 167). Such functions begin as a spontaneous, subjective necessity but possess also their own value which allows them to be independent of the subject. The desire of rationalism to

divorce culture from life is mistaken, for "there is no culture without
life, no spirituality without vitality, in the most down-to-earth sense
of that word" (III, 168). Ortega aimed to reintegrate culture and the
spontaneous vitality from which it springs.

Life, then, is a tension between the purely biological and the
spiritual impulses. By means of this system of checks and balances, a
healthy relationship must be established so that life is culture and
culture is vital. Ortega preferred the traditionalist's mystical cultural
prejudices to the rationalist's insincere adherence to ideas that are
mere objective imperatives which no longer live and thus no longer
inspire faith. Such an attitude has converted culture into "a surface
fiction on top of effective life" (III, 171), a tissue of past ideas in which
we only think we believe. The "failure of culture" to which postwar
Europeans liked to refer was, according to Ortega, rather a failure of
European vitality that had allowed culture to wither through a lack of
vital stimulation.

Socrates made the great European discovery by isolating reason
and seeing it as the key to an unchanging universe governed by the
laws of concepts. However, he also supplanted what we are spontaneously with the secondary reality of reason. In the twentieth
century it is possible to see where he erred: "Pure reason cannot
supplant life: the culture of the abstract intellect is not, when com-
pared with spontaneous culture, another self-sufficient life that can
dislodge the first. *It is only a tiny island floating on the sea of primary
vitality*" (III, 177). Europe in this century finds itself at the end of the
line begun by Socrates and must once more submit culture and
reason to the demands of life: "Pure reason must surrender its authority to vital reason" (III, 178). It must be recognized that an object has a
dual existence in that it consists of certain real properties, plus unreal
elements, or values. [5] Whereas the former may be perceived by such
faculties as the intellect or the senses, the latter depend on our
estimative faculty, which manifests itself in our preferences. These,
in turn, are necessarily of a hierarchical system. As a result, the value
attributed to life itself is of enormous importance. Since the
eighteenth century, however, the value of life had been seen to lie
only in the service to such abstractions as the Good, the Beautiful, and
the True, which have in effect been deified. Culture, like the possession of God in an earlier period, had become something always
beyond man's reach, and thus Ortega saw modern "culturalism" as
another form of utopianism, progressivism, and futurism. The
danger, he believed, lay in attitudes that elevated certain vital activi-

ties while scorning others, and he demanded that the totality and indivisibility of life become the supreme value: "Life imposes on all its activities an imperative of wholeness, and whoever says 'yes' to one of them must affirm them all" (III, 186).

The value of life is intrinsic to it, but modern philosophies have contributed to the inversion of values by concentrating exclusively on that "other" which is not life, but with which it is constantly occupied. Ortega, however, saw the other as merely an excuse created by vitality and to which it gives value through its ability to prefer and to feel enthusiasm for what is superior. This recognition by our age of the value of life itself, so often considered sinful by Christianity, had Goethe and Nietzsche as its prophets, yet Ortega found European man still disoriented. He had lost his previous system of values (God and Culture) and had not yet adjusted to the new vitalistic perspective of his circumstance. What used to be central had been relegated to the periphery of the estimative hierarchy and its place was being taken by spontaneity and a lack of seriousness. Such a realignment toward the sportive and festive sense of life meant that life derived its value from spontaneous enthusiasm for an undertaking.

In the final chapter, "The Doctrine of the Point of View," Ortega summed up and explicated his perspectivism. Going beyond the theories of both rationalism and relativism, he saw the subject as a sort of sieve that has as its function the choosing and understanding of certain truths, and a perceptual blindness to others. This is likewise the psychic structure of the individual, the generation, the people, and the time. It is perspective, an integral part of reality, of which it is the organization. There is no world, but rather a series of horizons peculiarly perceived through individual spontaneity: "Whole truth is obtained only by linking what my neighbor sees with what I see, and so on" (III, 202). This new orientation is the destiny of the twentieth century, the result of our organism and our circumstance; we must accept it and remain true to it. This is the theme of our time.

The book also includes three appendices that are further definitions of the concerns of the new times. In "The Decline of Revolutions," a contribution to his theories of the rhythms of history,[6] Ortega detected three essential moments in the complete historical cycle of a people. The first is dominated by the traditional spirit when men remain true to the lessons of their ancestors, rather than trust to their own judgment. It is a time of few great figures, before the appearance of individuality, when the authority of tradition and the wisdom of the collectivity seem to promise greater security. When the spirit of individuality does begin to develop, it represents an attempt to create something new that justifies independence from the collectivity. Such a creation is governed not by tradition, but by reason, and rationalist periods are the most glorious moments of the intellect when man's new theories and his discovery of his own inner laws make him feel divine. His faith in pure reason, when transferred to politics, nourishes revolutions, which are life put at the service of ideas. Ortega found the flaw in such an attitude in its utopianism, framing an idea "without any object other than that of perfecting it as an idea, regardless of how much it may conflict with reality" (III, 218). The almost inevitable failure of such utopias and the consequent disillusionment bring about the no less inevitable reaction of the equally utopian counterrevolution. When both programs reveal their rigidity in comparison with the richness of spontaneous life, the revolutionary period fades away and politics moves from the center of life to its periphery, as was then occurring in Europe.[7]

In the brief "Epilogue on the Disillusioned Soul," he gave some indication of the nature of the mystical spirit that characterizes the third stage in the historical cycle. It is a period of demoralization that, "after a fleeting moment of apparent splendor" (III, 228), becomes decadent. The loss of spontaneous faith after the failure of the utopias undermines man's courage to face the challenges of his destiny. Abstract values become meaningless, life seems arbitrary and man looks to anything in the hope of finding something to hold on to: "Perhaps the name that best suits the spirit that appears after the decline of revolutions is the term servile" (III, 230).

"The Historical Significance of Einstein's Theory" is an attempt to demonstrate the parallels between new modes of contemporary thought and Einstein's theory of relativity, "the most important intellectual fact that the present can show" (III, 231). Einstein's thought was to the present what Descartes's thought had been for the Modern Age.[8] Einstein's and Ortega's thoughts deny certain traditional absolutes and recognize that certain realities are perceived differently, according, in Einstein's case, to the frame of reference, and in Ortega's, to the observer. This knowledge of reality is true and thus absolute, whereas reality itself is relative and not merely a part of eternal truth that can be discovered deep within oneself. Einstein saw that man is only a part of the universe and not the center as rationalists held. Ortega dismissed as "provincialism" such a belief that a corner could be the center and reaffirmed his theory that perspective, rather than a merely subjectivist interpretation, is an integral and organizing element of reality; not a deformation, but an objective value in itself. Once more he rejected utopianism with the comment that "in the cosmic show there is no spectator without a definite seat" (III, 237). Thus, both time and space have a value as factors of reality. Einstein set limits on the universe by putting the abstractness of geometry at the service of matter in the belief that pure reason is not an absolute value but an instrument that must continually justify itself. Of course, this corroborated Ortega's own interpretation of the proper relationship betwen ideas and politics, culture and spontaneous life, for infinity loses its position as a governing principle and the universe will henceforth be seen as limited and closed.

CHAPTER 4

Ratiovitalism

I   *Ortega and the Dictatorship*

ORTEGA'S role as an intellectual leader and a social force was fully realized in the 1920s, a decade in which he published the works that gave him fame abroad, as well as a constant stream of political and philosophical essays. These years also saw the increasing power of *El Sol,* the creation of a nucleus for young intellectuals in the *Revista de Occidente,* founded only two months before the coup d'état, and a second triumphant visit to South America. Despite, or even because of, an almost absurd political situation, it was in these years that Ortega most nearly achieved his goal of raising Spain to the level of intellectual life in France, Germany, and Britain.

In the year preceding the declaration of the Dictatorship, he had pointed out elements in the current situation that would later be exploited by others to justify the need for a suspension of parliamentary democracy, and much of his terminology found its way into Primo de Rivera's manifesto of September 1923 and later government statements. As he had demonstrated in *Invertebrate Spain,* the country was suffering from "particularism," and Parliament could not avoid reflecting this. Parliament needed reform, he insisted, and rather optimistically he believed that two years of unhindered operation would allow the machine to perform again as it should. However, in a more immediate context, he had contemplated with chilling accuracy the near future:

It is very possible—more so than the abstractionists of democracy suppose—that at some time the need for a dictatorship will impose itself, not only in Spain, but likewise in France, Italy, Germany. That this possibility may be discerned is perhaps the most significant feature of the period that is now beginning in Europe. Well, dictatorships have only been able to be born in Parliaments. From them they have received the electric charge that their transitory and all-embracing authority requires. (XI, 23; 1922)

Hitler was a decade from power, Mussolini was still a largely unknown quantity, and Primo de Rivera would change the destiny of Spain in just over fourteen months.

The politics of the military dictatorship was generally hostile to free intellectual activity, in which the government perceived a constant threat. To a large extent, such an attitude reflected the insecurities of the king, who had been subjected to frequent attacks by liberal intellectuals, and of Primo de Rivera himself, who preferred a loutish form of censorship, riddled with inconsistencies. While not an intrinsically evil regime, it was unworthy of its time and of a great modern nation, although it did succeed in imposing a sort of order that permitted the country to lurch along for another six and one-half years. Few voices of protest were heard within the country, and the most vigorous attacks were launched from abroad, where many liberals, including Unamuno, Blasco Ibáñez, and even Eduardo Ortega y Gasset, found themselves, either voluntarily or by government decree.[1]

Against such a backdrop, Ortega became the preeminent intellectual figure in Spain, not as Maeztu did, by collaborating with the policies of the government, to which he was more or less resigned, but rather by writing around the restrictions imposed. Immediately after the establishment of the Dictatorship, he wrote proportionally less about national politics for reasons that are difficult to assess. However, the fear of seeing the closure of his newly founded *Revista de Occidente* cannot be discounted as a serious consideration. It was not until some two months after the coup that he made any public comment about the new situation, and even that was mild in tone. For the entire life of the Dictatorship, many of his works seemed not to deal with the immediate situation, but rather to aim at values that transcended daily political problems. Nonetheless, all these works contributed to the creation of a new, more flexible Spanish mentality, for which the great problems of politics and social behavior were kept alive.

It must be stated that, however much the form of the military government may have offended him, Ortega expressed considerable sympathy for its declared objectives. In this, his initial position was not unlike that of other intellectuals, exasperated by the previous chaos, but while many of them came to see that the government's actions were less noble than the manifesto had promised, Ortega avoided direct criticism. Nevertheless, he was not sure that the "old politics" against which the new regime was taking aim was precisely the same as that which he had attacked nearly a decade earlier. The weakness of the political system had made government by force all but inevitable, and he laid the blame squarely on the liberals, who had failed to seize their opportunity. Their tactics had consisted of an irresponsible emotional reaction to every problem, but their lack of realism had prevented them from coming forward with any useful proposals for reform. Only the Socialists, he felt, showed any trace of being able to discern the patterns of the future. Consequently, he was led to the discouraging conclusion that, for the vast majority who casually preferred to blame the politicians for everything that was wrong, the Dictatorship's promise to rid the country of the old politicians suggested a blissful release. Indeed, as he had commented earlier: "The important thing is not to punish the abuses of those who govern, but to replace the habits of those who are governed. . . . However detestable the 'old politicians,' much worse are the old Spaniards, the great inert and evil-tongued mass without impetus, fervor or internal discipline" (XI, 30–31; 1922). This mass antedated the new political structure and could be lulled but not reformed by sweeping away members of the old regime. The Dictatorship, then, could easily be guilty of merely catering to this widespread irresponsibility.

Whatever its other drawbacks, the new political reality offered Spain the chance to begin anew. Ortega believed that a certain amount of imposition is unavoidable in responsible government and he gradually developed a series of concrete proposals for the regeneration of the country, based on "liberty and authority" (XI, 81; 1925). By 1926, he was convinced that both Bolshevism and Fascism were illusory solutions and historical aberrations that Spain could and must avoid in search of a new path: "The world has become soft again and ready to take on a new shape . . . . Let us try a new form of Spanish life, leaner, more energetic, more elegant, more historical. Let us feel the proud urge to reenter history, to place a hand on it and create destiny. It is the right moment" (XI, 93; 1926). Behind his lofty vocabulary, Ortega was calling for a far more realistic approach than any previously attempted.

II   Toward a Revitalized Politics

Ortega sought to extract from political history lessons that could be applied to contemporary Spanish needs.[2] In a series of articles published in El Sol in January and February 1927 he looked upon the figure of Mirabeau as a model of the supreme politician, a creature whose nature he wished to define, more as a type of vitality than as a historical symptom. He found in him a man whose destiny it was to recognize the historical appropriateness of the principle of constitutional monarchy and to champion it until it was seen as an inescapable necessity. As Ortega observed: "his politics was so clear that the continent could follow no other for a century" (III, 618), yet his political sense was merely the final product and thus of secondary interest to Ortega who attended rather to the kind of vitality that makes possible the imposition of such a man on decades of European history. He found in Mirabeau a particular life force, the "magnanimous soul," for whom "the supreme delight is the frantic effort to create things" (III, 610), a man replete with "creative virtues" who feels himself transformed by a mission, a duty, a calling that goes beyond the limitations of the small, bourgeois, "negative" virtues within which the lesser, "pusillanimous" man plays out his comparatively feeble existence. In discussing such creators, such terms as egoism and altruism must be set aside, for this distinction "loses meaning when referred to the great man, because his 'ego' is full to the top with 'the other': his *ego* is an *alter*—the work. To be concerned about himself is to be concerned about the Universe" (III, 610).

Mirabeau was marked by an impulsiveness that allowed him to recognize and take advantage of opportunity, regardless of normal ethical standards. Since his vitality demanded action, he was never still, never dreamed or imagined, but simply *did*, and as a result, revealed himself as necessarily unscrupulous. However, as Ortega pointed out, "genius of this type rests on a basis of certain organic conditions that would seem monstrous in isolation, and without which there is no great political man" (III, 623). The man of action, of whom the politician is indeed the best example, lives necessarily projected into and fused with that which he is called upon to do. Since he lacks the intimate center that can be called a self, his ego being one with his work, he is unable to see it or respect it in others. Hence, the charges of immorality. In sum, "impulsiveness, turbulence, hystrionism, lack of precision, poverty of intimacy, thickness of skin, are the organic, elemental conditions of a political genius" (III, 625). Mirabeau was attuned to and dominated his vital horizon by postulating a future that demanded a true democracy. This "historical intuition" was all that was necessary to him, but, to have it, his mind had been sharpened through constant attention to other, apparently superfluous concerns, in his irresistible need to remain active, even while in prison or in exile. The key was his underlying vitality.

In the same year as his series on Mirabeau, Ortega gave voice to his
most specific proposals for political reform. The series of thirteen
articles, published in *El Sol* between January 1927 and February
1928, displays some of the difficulty of going beyond political abstractions at the moment when "the Dictatorship dictated with most
vigor," and when "a violent silence weighed on Spain" (XI, 175; 1931).
Although he was particularly concerned about what would follow the
Dictatorship, which could be only a temporary response, he cau-
tiously avoided the most controversial problem of all: the matter of
monarchy versus republic. Only in the introduction to the book,
published three weeks before the declaration of the Republic, did he
state that "the most immediate cause of Spain's misfortune is the
monarchy" (XI, 176; 1931).

The axis of his thought was still the total reorganization of Spain
through an imaginative balancing of the powers of local autonomy and
centralism, a project that he hoped would finally lead Spain into the
dazzling future that he felt should now be hers. Despite the deep-
rooted fear of change that locked her into a cautious mentality permit-
ting only small successes because it permitted only small experi-
ments, Spain was in a particularly malleable condition. Some social
stimulants had to be injected into the national bloodstream, not with
the aim of provoking a revolution, but to produce the kind of receptivity to her circumstance that makes possible a fruitful revolutionary
mentality, for "Spain has to conquer the average level of human life of
the time in which we are living" (XI, 195). The competent minority
had to attract the interest of the majority, demand its full participation and bring about the creation of "a more active, more capable,
more alert Spaniard" (XI, 198). Obviously, such a citizen could not be
a product of the capital alone, but must also come from the provinces
which had to be seen as an indispensable part of the whole. No longer
could the nation be confused with its center, for the life of the
provinces "is Spain herself" (XI, 200), and must be raised.

The Constitution of 1876 had given too much power to the central
government and Parliament. It was unreasonable, for example, to
expect parliamentarians, however well intentioned, to be able to
understand fully even the smallest of local affairs, all of which necessarily fell to them to be judged. Moreover, the only electors for whom
government had any immediate reality were those who lived in
Madrid and, to a lesser extent, the other major urban areas. Since
about three-quarters of the deputies were elected from the smaller
provincial centers and the rural areas, Parliament could scarcely

avoid finding itself severely hindered by the distance between the concrete interests of the majority of its members and the abstract character of the majority of its concerns.

As a consequence, rural Spaniards had generally withdrawn from the electoral process, leaving a political vacuum that could be filled only by *caciquismo* and organized elections. Ortega did not consider this to be an abuse of the Constitution, but said rather that "it was the only way to carry out the Constitution" (XI, 220). Yet, the result was that people were elected, not with the purpose of serving in a Parliament that was in any case irrelevant to them, but in order to accumulate real power at the local level where it mattered. By 1900, the local organizations had become so demanding that the central government was forced to cater to the worst kind of localism in order to obtain their support. When the local levels became more powerful than the central government, the Constitution was, in effect, ignored and invalidated, with the dangerous result that the government received the blame for dissatisfaction at the level where it really had no control. The only way to reestablish equilibrium and counteract the rebellion of the regions against Madrid, then, was gradually to involve people in rural areas in regional issues so that they would come to understand the role that they could play on the national level. For the rural areas, this meant an absolute increase in vitality, since "that local life is very local and very little life" (XI, 241). Still, it was virtually the only life that Spain had.

Clearly necessary was a new Constitution that must, on the one hand, separate legislative and executive power while, on the other, dividing the country into ten or twelve large regions, based on historical and geographical affinities, that would be autonomous in local matters. The local assemblies would be large, with one member for every ten thousand people, and all the major institutions and governmental operations would be gathered in a single city in each region, "in order to contribute to the creation of great regional capitals, potent and complete cities, which would have an indespensable role in raising the level of the average Spaniard" (XI, 259). The central government in Madrid would oversee the actions of these assemblies and attend to specific matters requiring a national perspective. The number of members of Parliament would be greatly reduced and Ortega hoped that the most competent people could be attracted so that they could attend to truly global problems. Clearly he hoped to perceive a future for Spain as clear as that which Mirabeau had seen for Europe.

III   *Ratiovitalism in Historical Study*

In an article published in the *Revista de Occidente* in October 1924 Ortega recognized that whereas it had previously been necessary "to seduce towards philosophical problems with lyrical means" (III, 270), the public was now better prepared to begin reading and dealing with philosophy on its own terms. "Ni vitalismo ni racionalismo" [Neither Vitalism nor Rationalism] is a clarification of some of the ideas outlined in *El tema de nuestro tiempo,* and an attempt to demonstrate that, while his concepts should not be understood as mere biologism, neither should they be seen as undermining the importance of reason. Rather, they were directed against rationalism as a philosophical dogmatism that aimed to cast the world in its own image.

Once more finding his roots in Plato, Ortega observed that reason is a knowledge that leads to the innermost depths of an object, "beyond the manifest and apparent" (III, 273), and permits the breaking down of the object into its essential elements so that we seem to see it from within itself (a principle he was to apply to biography): "Strictly speaking, rationality means that movement of reducing and can be considered synonomous with defining" (III, 274). However, reason necessarily exhausts itself upon reaching the irreducible elements of the object. These can be known only by intuition, which is clearly "illogical, irrational, since it excludes the proof or reason" (III, 275). At this point reason becomes mere contemplation and rationalism reveals itself as a limited and insufficient tool, capable only of a reality contingent upon our ideas. Leibniz could respond only by inquiring if the concept thus reached was possible, that is, whether it contained any contradiction. Yet here again, Ortega found that the answer could be based only on intuition, for the mere absence of contradictions still permits incongruities which intuition can reject, but which reason alone cannot disprove. Leibniz took refuge in the concept of an infinite reason, situated in God, and distinct from the limited intellect of man, but Ortega saw that this, too, was an irrational concept. The conclusion seemed clear: first, that "reason is a brief zone of analytical clarity that opens between two unfathomable layers of irrationality"; and second, that the reductive character of reason leads it inescapably to "an intuitive method, opposed to it, but from which it lives. Reasoning is a pure combining of unreasonable visions" (III, 277). This is its proper function; anything more is mere rationalism, an arbitrary belief that the behavior of things is identical to that of our ideas; hence, idealism.

The irrational nature of the mathematical and physical sciences was fast becoming a legitimate concern in those fields and it was no longer enough to assume that that which is unknown to us behaves in the same way and following the same laws as that which is known. Indeed, Ortega shrewdly observed that what we know may be the only things that do behave in such a manner, in which case idealism and rationalism blind us to various strata of reality, imposing upon them a logical but subjective way of being that demands that things conform to our ideals. Such an inversion means that reality ceases to be the goal and becomes rather the methodological starting point. Instead, Ortega saw life as the basis for all coherent thought, and inseparable from it.

Throughout this period he continued to display an attentiveness to the significance of the supposedly frivolous and irrational elements in human life. His sportive theory of life was taking form in several essays of the period,[3] and in *Las Atlántidas* [The Atlantises, 1924] he considered the scheme of preferences of an age as facets of permanent dimensions of spiritual life, controlled by strict, but still largely unknown, laws. Surely, he argued, our preferences spring from a more intimate and vital force in our being than reason, which is, after all, essentially conventional and restricted in its scope. To illustrate his point, he chose the current European interest in remote periods and civilizations, which did far more to stimulate enthusiasm than the more practical problems of postwar reconstruction, from which they may indeed have served as a respite. In fact, this was simply an extension of a spontaneous enthusiasm that, in the last quarter-century, had expanded the human horizon toward a greater awareness of Far Eastern civilizations, of the ethnography of primitive peoples, of prehistory, and of the discovery of what he called "the Atlantises": those ancient cultures that had vanished from the historical horizon.[4]

It is difficult to imagine a more serious change in a civilization than a dramatic expansion of its "vital horizon," its temporal and geographical consciousness. Every aspect of life, including the most trivial, is in some measure a function of man's concept of and response to his vital horizon, his sense of the scope of the universe in which he lives. "Life is a dialogue with the surroundings" (III, 291), and no action can be understood if the sense of the surroundings within which it is realized is not understood as well. Extending his earlier perspectivism, Ortega pointed out that each species and generation has its own horizon, within which each individual has a more limited one that reflects the selection he has made, based on his point of view. To understand others, we must be able to understand the horizon in view of which they felt themselves to be functioning.

Just as expansions or contractions of the vital horizon bring with them shifts in a race's perception of its historical location, they may also cause severe dislocations in its perception of the relative importance of other activities in its culture. In his own time, Ortega saw the concept of culture broaden as it turned pluralistic and become biological as it was applied to all the higher functions of human life. Consequently, it was essential for the study of history to see the secondary phenomena as part of the complete organic structure that is culture, in which each element necessarily supposes the others. The new interest in ethnology, and especially the studies of Leo Frobenius (1873–1938) and Spengler, recognized cultures as the true protagonists of history. While disagreeing with the belief that cultures are sealed off from each other, Ortega did agree that "the intuition of universal pluralism, as a pure fact, as a phenomenon, is the great innovation in European culture" (III, 304). It was this change from the unitarianism of the last two centuries that injected totally unimagined possibilities into science as it applied to the plurality that it now saw and accepted, its desire to find unity. The further reality may well be unitarian, just as thought must be, "but it is necessary to leave open always the possibility that the facts will refuse to coincide with this ideal of unity that breathes within thought" (III, 304). Ortega predicted that, for at least a generation, a "polycentric" type of historical study would be cultivated, recognizing the existence of various "cultural ambits" which, when juxtaposed, "will form a panorama of human destinies rather like a cubist picture" (III, 307).

"Historical sense," an awareness of human cultural diversity, is the characteristic most necessary to the historian, who must be able to recognize not only external differences between periods and cultures, but also reject the assumption that the underlying man is essentially the same despite these differences. The twentieth century, Ortega argued, was more aware of the need not only to step back far enough to see how other times and cultures differ from ours, but also to move close enough to make sense of these divergencies. Consequently, he saw two directions in which historical study had to move: first, "the psychology of evolution," an intensified awareness of the variability of man through an ability to reconstruct human consciousness within different horizons: "the more radical this variety is admitted to be, the sharper the historical sense" (III, 311); and second, an increased ability to evaluate changes and potentiate the cultures they represent, whatever their location in time or space: "Then, and only then, will it be possible to say that there exists in Europe a discipline of Humanities" (III, 312). Each period and people would reveal its vital theme and enrich by its example. Simply to recognize the plurality and relativity is inadequate, for "history is historical reason, an effort and a tool to overcome the variability of historical material . . ." (III, 313). The new term, "historical reason," had been coined and would acquire an almost technical meaning as Ortega attempted a revolution in the philosophy of history.[5]

IV *Ratiovitalism in the Arts*

By bringing together the flow of the rhythms of European history with those of its philosophy and fine arts, Ortega believed important conclusions could be deduced regarding the evolution of the European spirit. In this way, each work of art became for him the crystallization of a given moment in which the point of view employed acquired a telling significance. He demonstrated his thesis in "Sobre el punto de vista en las artes" [On Point of View in the Arts], published in the *Revista de Occidente* in February 1924.

In its infancy, painting treated all objects alike, analytically, suggesting distance by means of size, but interpreting technically everything in the same way, with the result that every element could take on the role of center of interest. No unity or true visual hierarchy was established and the total painting was the sum of innumerable small works. Raphael subjected the painting to greater demands of composition, but the real transition began with the Venetians, and continued for the better part of a century, during which architectural unity began to be joined with effects of light and shade. The use of a single source of light, for example, imposed a new and real unity on the painting and represented a true point of view as light itself became an element of interest.

The mature Velázquez, however, represented for Ortega a genuine revolution, for he was the first to halt his pupil, and make the intervening air in which the objects seemed to float the center of interest; the totality of the painting had become the center. The Impressionists displaced the point of view into the artist himself, and painted the very act of seeing. Sensations and impressions were depicted: "Sensations are no longer in any sense things, but subjective states through which, by means of which, things appear to us"

(IV, 454). The point of view continued to approach the subject, until Cézanne and Cubism painted the ideas underlying the sensations. This permitted the appearance of purely psychic, "intrasubjective" realities as external objectivity and reference to it were gradually eliminated. The painter's eyes no longer received images, but rather projected them onto the canvas. The necessary consequence of artistic evolution, this progression from things to sensations to ideas found its parallel in the evolution of Western thought from the substantialist realism of Dante through Descartes and Leibniz to Idealism and Positivism.[6]

New ways of thinking, new responses to the changing vital horizon, are almost always seen in the arts. In *La deshumanización del arte* [The Dehumanization of Art], first published as articles in *El Sol* in 1924, Ortega looked at the extraordinary vitality of contemporary art which deliberately divided its public into two antagonistic camps: those who understood it, an especially gifted minority; and the mass who did not and in whom, as a consequence, it inspired deep resentment and hostility.[7] He noted that contemporary art "is an art of privilege, of nobility of nerves, of instinctive aristocracy" (III, 355). The bourgeois, the "mass man," felt excluded from the new artistic experience, while the "select man" found in it a stimulus for his sense of mission as part of a minority. Such a division heralded the new social divisions in which "the false supposition of real equality between men" (III, 356) would become evident, with sweeping results.

Ortega considered all the art of the nineteenth century realistic in the sense that it offered the viewer an opportunity to share and identify with the individual human experience set before him. Strictly speaking, however, this is not an aesthetic experience, for "the fact is that the artistic object is artistic only insofar as it is not real" (III, 358). Identification with the human subject matter, a characteristic of "popular" art, prevents the viewer from attending to the work of art itself. The early twentieth century, on the other hand, revealed as its distinctive tendency a movement toward "pure" art, stripped of those specifically human elements. The result was art for artists, for the initiated, "an artistic art" (III, 359), deliberately incomprehensible to the great majority. A new aesthetic sensitivity, a true feeling of disgust for the human element, manifested itself in "the tendency to dehumanize art" (III, 364). It was no longer possible to treat the world of art as an extension or facet of the viewer's world. The new response was truly and purely aesthetic as art moved deliberately away from human reality by overcoming it, while still requiring it as a point of reference: "The aesthetic pleasure for the new artist emanates from this triumph over the human; for this reason it is necessary to make the victory concrete and to present in every case the strangled victim" (III, 366). Avoidance of the mere reproduction of reality demanded exceptional gifts so that conventional, personal reality did not reassert its hold.

All confessional aspects seemed aesthetically fraudulent to the new artists. The artistic experience was no longer to be based upon a heated mechanical reaction to the feelings and experiences of the artist, a "psychic contagion" (III, 369), but rather upon cool, luminous understanding, an ascending movement of the spirit. New poets—unlike the Romantics, who wanted to display their most private emotions—wanted simply to invent, to create and conquer new territory which did not already reverberate with human sensations. A newly created reality had become the center of art: "Poetry today is the superior algebra of metaphors" (III, 372). The metaphor had become substantive, not only as a potent tool for the escape from existing reality, but also as the weapon to denigrate and destroy it, "the most radical instrument of dehumanization" (III, 374). Ideas were being taken for the essential unreality that they are and this unreality was objectivized and made real. Painting depicted the very idea that the artist had of his subject, "the delicious fraud of art" (III, 377).

Art was no longer intended to be sacred or eternal; highly ironical and informed by a spirit of self-mockery, self-destruction was its permanent feature. It carried man back to a childlike exuberance, closely related to the spirit of games and the cult of eternal youth that had sprung up in postwar Europe. As a result of a changing "biological rhythm," art, like science and politics, had moved from the center of man's enthusiasm to the periphery, where it was free of some of its responsibilities and pretensions. The results were still scarce, and while Ortega stopped short of endorsing the new attitude, he recognized that it demanded understanding, for there could be no turning back.[8]

Ideas sobre la novela [Ideas on the Novel], which first appeared in *El Sol* in December 1924 and January 1925, is to no small degree an application to a specific genre of the more general aesthetic approaches contained in *The Dehumanization of Art*. Despite its brevity, it remains an important commentary on the state of the art and was, on Ortega's side, the final stage in the polemic with Pío Baroja, which had lasted for some fifteen years. Since he considered the novel to be the most characteristic literary form of the nineteenth century, it was natural that he should make an attempt to understand it as an integral expression of the vital horizon of his time. Moreover, the "crisis of the novel" was very much a topic in literary circles at the time, and Ortega and Baroja had stimulated the discussion in Spain. Ortega attributed the apparent decline of the novel as an expressive vehicle to two causes. First, he saw every genre as containing only a limited number of possibilities and the novel, quite simply, had run out of themes. The second problem was that, in its early stages, "novel" had meant "novelty," but decades of novels, including many great ones, had caused public taste to evolve to the point where it demanded far more complex works than in the past. The vital horizon had altered so that new techniques and finer quality ingredients were needed to restore authentic presence to the novel, thus making less important the novelty of the subject matter.

Because contemporary readers knew so much more about psychology, novels from a more innocent time now seemed unconvincing. The "imaginary psychology" of literary characters offered the richest potential for the genre: "Not in the invention of 'actions,' but in the invention of interesting souls do I see the best future for the novelistic genre" (III, 418). The reader must feel that he is in direct contact with the characters, whom he must discover living and developing; he must sense them coming into being, and the great novelist will place his reader in the position from which he can experience this for himself. As Ortega had already demonstrated in the *Meditations on Quixote*, what is important is not what happens, or to whom, but rather the way in which it is presented and made of interest to the reader. Now the novelist must develop a "presentative" approach to achieve this and galvanize the genre by recapturing the imagination of the reader and requiring his participation. Therefore, the novel must be slow, almost leisurely, so that the reader has an opportunity to mix with the characters, for he will always remember the great characters more vividly than their adventures.

Ortega believed that adventure could be nothing more than a necessary pretext in the novel, as could be seen in the works of Dostoevsky, who gave greater density to his generally simple plots by means of a slow and skillful development and an almost classical use of limited temporal and spatial elements. As in life, his characters do not readily surrender their secrets, and the reader senses their "reality" precisely because the novelist uses his technique to disorient him as the characters' actions fail to correspond fully to what the reader had expected.[9] In this way, the reader is forced to create his own definition of each character. Although Proust also recognized the importance of almost sluggish development, Ortega found that his "paralytic" work tended to lack that essential fiber of minimal dramatic interest. A balance must be struck, then, between action, which Ortega considered as dead weight in aesthetic terms, but essential to focus the reader's attention, and atmosphere, far more enduring and suitable for contemplation, but which by itself lacks dynamism.

The novelist must cut the reader off from his "real" vital horizon and surround him with beings who could not be part of his daily existence. This new, closed horizon must contain its own potential to vibrate with interest so that, upon finishing a novel, the reader may have the sensation of reemerging from a different world, "and the novel that cannot achieve it will be a bad novel, whatever its remaining virtues" (III, 410). This imprisonment of the reader requires, of course, "a generous plenitude of details" (III, 414) that give the impression that there is always more to be discovered. Since we must forget our external reality, Ortega rejected "political, ideological, symbolic or satirical" novels (III, 411), for they retain too solid a link that constantly drags the reader back to daily life. The novel must be hermetic, impenetrable, and intranscendent. Art must not aim to be anything else as well. If all that his analysis sets forth are the minimal requirements for the twentieth-century novel, Ortega nonetheless considered that this period of decay had returned the novel to its proper function and that the time was right for the creation of the perfect novel, the culmination of decades of experience that had served to establish a clear difference between good novels and bad. Rather than predict the imminent disappearance of the novel, he believed that "the ultimate perfection" (III, 416) was still to come.

V *Philosophical Anthropology*

Ortega's vitalism needed the support of a clear understanding of the functions of the psyche. He had frequently expressed dissatisfaction with the lack of precision in contemporary psychology and it was to be expected that he would try to cast new light on a field that had reached a stage of crisis by the 1920s and had captured nearly everyone's interest, as even a glance at the contents of the *Revista de Occidente* will prove. Ortega had first read Freud in 1911 as he began to emerge from the overwhelming influence of Hermann Cohen, and later had his works translated into Spanish. Despite his own misgiv-

ings about Freud's theories, he wrote in his prologue to the translation: "The ideas of Freud have, in fact, been the most original and
suggestive creation that has crossed the horizon of psychiatry in the
last twenty years" (VI, 301; 1922). Nonetheless, he found the theories
too mechanistic, and in an article written in May 1925 he attempted to
reverse them with his own analysis of the inner reaches of the
psyche.[10] Clearly, the traditional division between body and soul was
no longer acceptable and Ortega's own theories of vital reason did not
permit such an arbitrary separation, as the body reclaimed its rightful
dignity, equal to that long accorded to the spirit: "The new era
advances with letters on its banners: 'One and the other.' Integration.
Synthesis. Not amputations" (II, 455). Moreover, modern psychology had made no serious attempts to give new precision to the word
"soul," in which the role of the body would be included. In
"Vitalidad, alma, espíritu" [Vitality, Soul, Spirit], Ortega's
"philosophical anthropology" set as its task the examination of the
psyche as revealed in the three facets mentioned in the title.

Vitality, the first and most basic segment, "is that portion of our
psyche that lives infused in the body" (II, 455), and is inseparable
from it. It is, "to some extent, subconscious, obscure and latent" (II,
462), since we have both internal and external knowledge only of our
body itself. Normally, the state of the "intrabody"[11] is never noted as
such, although the image and sensation that we have of it provide the
basis for both our psychic life and our external world. Ortega suspected that this image is radically different in each individual, and
intimately related to, for example, such determining traits as one's
characteristic optimism or pessimism. All our mental and physical
activities spring from this energy that we feel within ourselves, and
we are unavoidably affected by that which we sense in others. "All life
is contagious: corporal and spiritual" (II, 459), and we instantly sense
whether others have an abundance of vitality that stimulates us, or a
lack of it that exhausts us.

The other extreme of the psyche, the spirit, represents "the entirety of intimate actions of which anyone feels himself to be the true
author and protagonist" (II, 461). This is the volitional and intellectual
region. However, both vitality and the spirit clearly reveal themselves only in relation to the zone that lies between them: the soul,
"the region of the feelings and emotions, of the desires, of the
impulses and appetites" (II, 462), the region of spontaneous
movements that are not I, and upon which I look somewhat as a
spectator. Nonetheless, I control the relationship between my soul
and the other zones of my psyche, rendering any of the elements
more "hermetic" or "porous."

To each of these psychic regions Ortega attributed a "self." The spiritual self, although personal in the extreme, is that part of us that functions according to objective, cultural standards, and exists always in indissoluble reference to the universal and objective, where logic may rule. The self of the soul, however, may exist apart since sources of joy and pain differ for each individual and are ultimately intransferable. The vital self is related to heredity and the biology of the species and may, Ortega postulated, always represent a moment of a "universal vitality" and a "cosmic unity" (II, 468). Men are united then, in the body and spirit, but separated in the privacy of the soul. Each individual, each stage of life, each people, each historical period, represents a different admixture of vitality, soul, and spirit, one of which provides the principal foundation upon which it exists.

In July and August 1926 and July 1927 *Estudios sobre el amor* [Studies on Love], Ortega's major psychological essay of the period, appeared as articles in *El Sol*. It represents his most thorough development of a theme that reappeared throughout his work as he saw the relationship between the sexes and the choice of a beloved as indispensable elements that serve both to characterize the individual and contribute to a definition of his sense of purpose.[12] By way of introduction, Ortega defined his theme in the broadest and noblest sense, as *eros*, the compulsion in the soul that brings together the individual and every higher goal: "there is nothing as fertile in our intimate life as the amorous feeling; so much so that it becomes the symbol of all fertility" (V, 554). Insatiable and ever active, love is the great natural force that carries the individual beyond his own confines. It is the source of many emotional, spiritual, and intellectual impulses, and can be measured by the degree of suffering and pain that it can produce and withstand. Love begins as a result, initiated by a stimulus produced by an object, and then functions as a centrifugal movement from the lover toward the beloved. It displays many characteristics similar to those found in hatred, but "love flows in a warm corroboration of the beloved and hatred secretes a corrosive virulence" (V, 558). Love is a life-giving sharing of two intimacies in that it is an active and intentional affirmation and strengthening of the existence of the beloved; it is concord, whereas "hatred is discord, metaphysical dissent, an absolute not being with the hated object" (ibid.)

In "El amor en Stendhal" [Love in Stendhal] Ortega considered Stendhal's theories as expressed in *De l'Amour* (1822). However, he found Stendhal's drawing-room theories to be marred by an idealism that made of the beloved a projection of the lover, and by a pessimism rooted in the belief that love was a fiction that had to fabricate for the beloved perfections that reality did not recognize. Ortega dismissed both Stendhal's idea that love is a fraud and his claim that love's apogee is reached when it ends as indications that the love had been a mistake, and he rejected any suggestion that error could be a normal element of love. For Ortega love was, as it had been for Plato, a movement toward someone or something that exudes superiority, a perceived perfection that causes the lover to seek a union with the beloved. It is not mere sexual appetite, which can be readily satisfied, but neither does it exclude sexual union which embraces a wish to perpetuate the perceived perfection.

Stendhal's image of crystallization suggests a degree of heightened awareness in love, an augmentation, where Ortega found an elimination, as the limits of perception become greatly narrowed. Love's object is placed highest in a hierarchy of attentiveness in which it acquires greater importance, greater reality, and greater value as it occupies greater space in the lover's soul. Sadly, the process never varies: falling in love is in fact an inferior and mechanical spiritual process that effects a paralysis of the capacity for attending to other things. The beloved is not bestowed with fictitious perfections, but rather the lover's almost obsessive attention gives greater existence to those already present. Like mysticism, falling in love represented for Ortega spiritual anarchy, an emptying of the mind of everything save a single object that may eventually achieve union with the subject, thus effectively eliminating both subject and object and producing an undisciplined state in the soul. This is the "state of grace" common to the lover and the mystic, in which this world becomes unimportant and everything is bathed in the uncritical light of beatitude. Both live outside of this world and of themselves: *ex-stasis*. Rather than see mysticism as a sublimation of eroticism, Ortega saw both as parallel impulses springing from a common source.[13]

Neither rational nor voluntary, preference is the essential characteristic of love. Just as a man normally passes through two or three radical changes in his life, so will he love an equal number of times as each type of woman loved corresponds to his current way of sensing life. The tracing of this amorous trajectory casts light on the totality of his intimate evolution. Unlike that of the lower animals, man's sexual impulse is less a result of instinct than of his fantasy, a fact that Ortega believed explained the lesser sexuality of woman, whose soul is more of a piece and less given to fantasy than the masculine soul. As a result, women are usually less attracted by a man's physical beauty or any qualities of genius. The man that other men find interesting offers little appeal to women, for his attraction is masculine and rooted in the exceptional, whereas women are attracted by more routine virtues and mediocrity.

Ortega believed that the essentially quiet characteristics of woman were of greater social significance than the more exuberant postures of man, and that in each historical period and within each cultural circle a certain type of woman is always preferred. Likewise, each type of woman will prefer a certain type of man, whom she will consider to be worthy of her love. Even a slight readjustment from one period to another, when applied to a nation, for example, would cause profound changes in every structure of society. The type of woman that predominates in a given time or culture thus becomes one of the subtlest forces to be studied. Although the tension produced by outstanding figures is secondary to this quiet process of selection, it serves to raise the average and provide a counterbalance to the female tendency "to maintain the species within mediocre limits, to avoid selection in the sense of the very best, to manage to keep man from ever becoming a demigod or an archangel" (V, 626).[14]

It will be seen that Ortega's vision of female psychology is often expressed in a manner that provokes an emotional rather than an intellectual response in the reader. Nonetheless, as he pointed out, "the historian who wants to understand a period needs, above all, to establish a table of dominant values in the men of that time" (V, 599), and certainly the values that can be discerned in a vision of love are no less telling and powerful than those that govern politics or philosophy.

VI   ¿Qué es filosofía?

There was a discernible readjustment in Ortega's thought after 1927, the result, at least in part, of his reading of Martin Heidegger's *Sein und Zeit,* published that same year. Suddenly, the evolution of philosophy threatened to surpass Ortega as he found in another member of his generation many concepts disconcertingly similar or related to his own. Much as he had had to place a distance between himself and Unamuno in 1909, he now felt compelled to respond to Heidegger's implicit challenge. He began to modify greatly his concept of vitalism and spontaneity and to reveal a more urgent need to create a truly rigorous system. As a result, he all but abandoned the writing of philosophical essays until the years of his exile and instead concentrated on works that seemed to be more nearly finished.[15]

Certainly, he had created a new audience for serious philosophical discussion, yet by 1927 he had reached his intellectual maturity, with only the *Meditations on Quixote* as a substantial indication of his full capability. The impact of *Sein und Zeit* demonstrated the indispensability of his turning to the presentation of a complete system within which all his fragmentary thought could be lodged, on a level with the best in contemporary Europe. It was time for Ortega to meet his own standards for intellectual discipline.

¿Qué es filosofía? [What Is Philosophy?] was a consolidation of his thought and an indication of the direction his future works would take. Based on a series of eleven public lectures given in 1929, here is revealed his brilliant expository technique over an extended period of time. His instinct for intellectual organization is accompanied by an astute sense of his audience. The development of his points demonstrated an awareness that the more difficult ideas could not be reread and so he employed a method of encircling his target in an ever-tightening spiral. Each lecture began with a recapitulation of the ideas discussed to date, and gradually proceeded to the development of a still more important concept. As the series progressed, the lectures became denser, but he was always ready to make another swing around his prey, clarifying aspects of his development by means of an arresting metaphor. Ortega seduced his public; never condescending, but always lucid, he carried them along with him, irresistibly, toward an answer to the question enunciated in the title of the series.

His purpose was not to provide an introduction to philosophy, but rather "to take the philosophical activity itself, philosophizing itself, and submit it to a radical analysis" (VII, 279). After more than three centuries in which philosophy had allowed itself to be reduced to mere theory of the knowledge that only the physical sciences had seemed capable of discovering, these latter had expanded to the stage where they had to philosophize about themselves in order to attempt to resolve a crisis brought on by the awareness that they represent a symbolic and, therefore, secondary and inferior form of knowledge. Having discovered that it could not do everything, however, had become a source of renewed vitality for physics. Now, philosophy, too, could reassume its proper role as the means of discovering and understanding the totality of the Universe, an act of "intellectual heroism" (VII, 308) in which the philosopher sets out in search of the absolutely unknown and the potentially unknowable, filled with an "appetite for the Universe" (VII, 310). Rather than aim to provide concrete solutions to concrete problems, as is the destiny of science, philosophy answers that uniquely human need to know that distinguishes *homo theoreticus* from both God and the beast.

Philosophy must consider part of its duty to be the demonstration of the insolubility of certain problems as it searches for the first principles that are constitutionally beyond the reach of physical science.[16] It must always reexamine everything so as to discover "everything that there is" (VII, 319), regardless of whether it in fact exists. From the stump that we have, philosophy must try to discover the Whole, without even the certainty that the Whole is knowable, nor whether it is a Universe or a Multiverse. The world of which we are aware, like the forest in the *Meditations on Quixote*, is incomplete and has as its background all the things that we do not see, but whose absence we can sense and which philosophy attempts to make present. Only philosophy can have as its aim this absolute "other," for it is the only science that is truly autonomous in that it creates all its own suppositions. It is dedicated to that part of each thing that is universal, that makes it fit into the Whole, and so must achieve a communicable vision, a concept. It is the process of constant uncovering (*alétheia*) and saying: "if physics is everything that can be measured, philosophy is the whole of what can be said about the Universe" (VII, 342).

Ortega proposed an "absolute positivism" that would include intuitive evidence. In this way it would be possible to distinguish among three classes of things: "those that may be in the Universe, whether we know it or not; those that we erroneously believe there are, but which, in fact, there are not; and, finally, those that we can be sure that there are" (VII, 357–58). These last he called the "data of the Universe," for they can be neither doubted nor proven and are problematic only in that philosophy must begin by determining what they are.

Descartes began modern philosophy by systematically doubting the very existence of the outside world and recognizing that the unique characteristic of thought is that it is autogenous, independent of anything outside itself. Idealism took this to mean that external reality proceeds from thought, exists only as thought, and is thus contained within us. However, such a concept effectively seals us off from the outside world and leads to the discovery "that each self is, in its very essence, radical solitude" (VII, 374). Man's intimacy thus includes the Universe and cannot be penetrated by external reality. Such an idea could not satisfy Ortega, for if the self is the center of our

consciousness, then the external world, our "circumstance," forms
the periphery; yet he agreed with Idealism that only the thinking of
the thought, but not necessarily the object of the thought, is. Consequently, the external world is only when I think it; however, it is
neither my thought nor an independent reality: "Without objects
there is no subject" (VII, 402). This absolute coexistence of a self and
its world is living, the radical reality and philosophy's fundamental
problem. Being is "intimacy with oneself and with things" (VII, 408).

The new definition of life, then, means to be aware of our living as
an endless uncovering and a finding of ourselves in the world. Living
is what we do and what happens to us, a taking account of and
occupying ourselves with "the other," the world, the circumstance,
but with no physical or temporal distance between our life and our
world, no precedence of one over the other. This is our vital horizon,
which we cannot choose, but within which we can make certain
decisions: "Life is, at once, fatality and liberty, it is being free within a
given fatality. . . . We accept the fatality and within it we decide on a
destiny. Life is destiny" (VII, 431). Ortega thus began to touch upon
the dramatic, problematic quality of life by stressing that it is a
constant projection into the future, an endless series of decisions
regarding what we are going to be next, and attempts to preform that
future. Such decisions demand an awareness of what our life is and
the extreme mode of this is philosophy, "the attempt life makes to
transcend itself" (VII, 429).

VII   La rebelión de las masas [*The Revolt of the Masses*]

Ortega's most famous work, first published as articles in *El Sol*
between October 1929 and February 1930, had its origins in *Invertebrate Spain*. [17] Although it depends often on rhetoric, it is a lesson in
the inexorability of history that touched a continental nerve and gave
voice to a concern that was rapidly spreading throughout Europe.
The striking phenomenon of the postwar years, he observed, was that
the masses had risen to levels of influence and had established
themselves as a determining norm merely on the basis of quantity.
They had arrogated to themselves the right to perform any functions
they chose, simply because they saw no reason not to do so. Competency had ceased to be a consideration. The result was a "hyper-
democracy," unheard of in modern history, in which "the commonplace mind, knowing itself to be commonplace, dares to affirm

the rights of the commonplace and to impose them everywhere" (IV, 148), crushing individuality and excellence, and refusing to follow the lead of any qualified minorities. Every historical period has its own vital level, what Ortega called "the height of the times," and far from finding the twentieth-century decadent, he saw that the "vital repertory" of the average man, the possibilities easily within his reach, had attained a level that had previously been available only to the select minorities. The future was resplendent with potentiality. Contemporary man belonged to the world at large and, as Ortega had demonstrated in *Las Atlántidas*, this world had become extended both physically and temporally. The problem was that man was unsure of his goals. No directing minority provided purposes, with the result being "that strange duality of great power and insecurity that dwells in the contemporary soul" (IV, 168).

Ortega considered such uncertainty an essential stimulus that keeps man alert and vital, since in the face of the unprecedented wealth of opportunities, he is forced to make choices. However, he also saw that the attitude of mass-man does not lead him to choose, for although he had been given the polish of civilization by democracy and the technical development of the nineteenth century, his spirit had not been imbued with its dynamic forces or its sense of responsibility. History's spoiled child, he was lulled by the material ease of his life, which offered every promise of becoming still more unrestricted, and felt quite justified in taking his comfort for granted. The lack of external pressure made mass-man satisfied with his initial reaction to any situation, while for the select man, "life has no savor for him if he does not make it consist in service to something transcendental" (IV, 182). Constantly in search of improvement and challenge, the select man creates a life of nobility and discipline, and his privileges are the result of the excellence of his own efforts to surpass himself, unlike the universal and automatic rights enjoyed by lesser men.

Mass-man was a *Naturmensch*, living in and enjoying the fruits of a civilized world, but blind to their fragility and indifferent to their value. Even the man of science has become a mass-man, an expert in one field, but astonishingly and even willfully ignorant of almost all other aspects of life. The simple distinction between ignorance and wisdom had become clouded and the "learned ignoramus" (*sabio-ignorante*, IV, 218), sealed into self-satisfaction, believed himself to be qualified in everything. The very success of European civilization jeopardized its continuation, for Europe lacked leaders abreast of the times, prepared to direct the reconstruction of her increasingly complex civilization, the technical progress of which outstripped the spiritual advancement of her citizens.

The rebellion of the masses was, quite simply, an evasion, a revolt against their destiny, against any external authority. The "New Adam" neither listened nor discussed; his "ideas" rested upon no authority beyond himself. Herein lay the cause of the new barbarianism, for "there is no culture where there is no respect for certain ultimate intellectual positions to which one may refer in a dispute" (IV, 188–89). The political form of such attitudes was seen in the rapidly developing Fascist and Syndicalist movements, which gave life to the principle of direct action, not as a final recourse when reason has been exhausted, but as a norm unto itself that weakens the relations of civilization and leads to dissociation. The inescapable result was violence, "the rhetoric of the times" (IV, 222). Ortega saw it elevated into the state itself which had become an awesome force, magnificent in its potential, but also an instrument that mass-man could look upon as his own because, like him, it was anonymous. He believed that all ills could be set right by the intervention of the state and this, in Ortega's view, was the greatest danger: "the stratification of life, the interventionism of the state, the absorption of all social spontaneity by the state; that is to say, the nullification of historical spontaneity which, in short, sustains, nourishes and impels human destinies" (IV, 225). As in the "false dawns" (IV, 205) of Bolshevism and Mussolini's Fascism, individuals are reduced to fodder for the state. Ortega saw this as merely a higher form of violence, made possible when the state became unlimited.[18]

For three centuries Europe had ruled the world but now she, and by extension other peoples, were beginning to display uncertainty regarding the leadership of the present and the future. This gave lesser nations and cultures the feeling that they had been unshackled, unleashing the exaggerated nationalisms that had broken out in the early part of this century. The spirit of mass-man was transported to the level of entire peoples who, while joyously declaring the bankruptcy of European standards, were incapable of creating others to replace them. An interregnum had begun.[19]

In *La misión de la universidad* [The Mission of the University, 1930], Ortega undertook a reexamination and redefinition of one of the social institutions of Europe that seemed not to be abreast of the times, and made concrete proposals for reforming it so as to meet the needs of the twentieth century. He discerned in the contemporary university three major defects, all of which were to some extent the legacy of the social perceptions of the nineteenth century. The most obvious was the comfortable, bourgeois origin of the majority of its students. If the level of national life was to rise, it was necessary to throw open the university to all those who could and should benefit from it, and especially the children of the working class. This meant, however, that the mass mentality so evident in society should not dictate the mission of the university.

The second defect was that he perceived that the nineteenth century had committed the university to two tasks that differed in both nature and purpose: the teaching of intellectual professions and the fostering of and training for scientific research. Although contemporary culture derives a great deal from the sciences, of which it is the necessary interpretation, a distinction must be made between culture, which aims to explain and give direction to life, and those aspects of science that are technical in nature. "General culture" was necessary for all students, but training for research could be of value only to an especially gifted minority. The nucleus of scientific activity is not vital nor does it respond to vital necessities, whereas culture is *"the plan of life*, the road map through the jungle of existence" (IV, 343). It was Ortega's conviction that the university's principal duty was to provide students with the repertory of vital concepts necessary to keep abreast of the times into which they were thrust.

Each man's reactions and decisions for his vital project are conditioned by the ideas of his time, within which there exists a stock of comfortable, outdated ideas, as well as a system that represents "the superior level of the time" (IV, 342) and to which the university must address itself. Excessive specialization, with an eye to social usefulness, had become the scourge of the twentieth century, but Ortega insisted that the man who was to take a role in the development of his society could not be considered competent if he did not also possess a reasonable awareness of the level of achievement and the most important concepts in areas of intellectual activity beyond his own: "Culture is the system of living ideas that each time possesses. Rather: the system of ideas *from* which the time lives" (IV, 341). Without this, even his attitudes within his own field must be called into question. As Ortega had said in *The Revolt of the Masses*, the contemporary fragmentation of European society could, to no small extent, be attributed to the growing domination of unidimensional man, ignorant of everything that does not appear to concern him personally. It was the task of the university "to reconstruct with the scattered pieces—*disiecta membra*—the vital unity of European man" (IV, 325).

This led Ortega to the third defect and the heart of his concern. The very existence of a university presupposes the existence of an "average" man, but it is obvious that such a man cannot hope to learn everything that the university aims to teach him. The university had tacitly accepted the failure inherent in the abyss that yawned between its pretensions and its achievements, and this falseness had become its very essence. It seemed clear, then, that the most radical and beneficial reform lay in "pedagogical economy," teaching only what can be learned. The material to be taught should be determined by the capacity of the student, as learner. The "tropical jungle of teachings" (IV, 332) demanded harsh pruning. The university should be returned to the students and these, seen as "average men," should be taught the strict minimum of things necessary for their lives and only insofar as these things can be learned fully and comfortably. Professional training must be based on the formation of a rigorous intellectual discipline, but while the training of scientific principles should be retained for all, the exercise of scientific research should be removed from the central concerns of the university, for Ortega saw all scientific research as an essentially creative vocation of which the average man is incapable. It is neither necessary, realistic, nor desirable to foster the illusion that each man must become a creative researcher. Rather, "an ingenious pedagogical rationalization would permit a more efficient and rounded teaching of the professions, in less time and with much less effort" (IV, 339).

To rectify the situation, he proposed as the core of the reformed university the creation of a "Faculty of Culture" wherein five "great cultural disciplines" would be taught, each of which would be supported by a strict scientific discipline. These would be:

1. The physical image of the world (Physics).

2. The fundamental themes of organic life (Biology).

3. The historical process of the human species (History).

4. The structure and operation of social life (Sociology).

5. The plan of the Universe (Philosophy). (IV, 335).

Such a change would give rise to a greater ability to synthesize, to understand in human terms, and to communicate knowledge, by making clear that part of science is essential to all. This would serve to humanize the scientist so that he would cease being "a barbarian who knows a great deal about one thing" (IV, 347), but it would require the development of a systematic pedagogical methodology that would organize knowledge: *"endow it with a form that is compatible with the human life that made it and for which it was made"* (IV, 348). Herein, he insisted, lay not only the future of the university, but also that of the sciences that otherwise would become so removed from man that they would cease to interest him.

A dynamic relationship, however, has to be established between the university, as stronghold of cultural and professional formation, for the average student, and centers of scientific investigation, for the better students who would be in contact with qualified researchers and especially gifted teachers. Both organisms are indispensable and interdependent: "Science is the *dignity* of the University; still more . . . , it is the *soul* of the University, the very principle that gives it life and keeps it from being only a base mechanism" (IV, 351–52). Likewise, the university must be open to its time and its society and be a vital part of both, a true "spiritual power," and a directing force in history.[20]

CHAPTER 5

Toward Historical Reason

I *Ortega and the Republic*

WITHIN days of the fall of Primo de Rivera in January 1930, Ortega began to attack the causes of the Dictatorship and to call for a national party that would dedicate itself to restoring "judicial dignity" to Spain. On November 15, 1930, he declared that the establishment of a new government under General Berenguer, with the intention of reestablishing political normalcy in the country, "'as if' nothing *radically* new, *substantially* abnormal had happened here" (XI, 277), was further evidence of the monarchy's intolerable cynicism. It revealed a belief, largely correct, that Spaniards were lacking in civic consciousness, but rather than attempt to rectify such a situation, as was its duty, the monarchy preferred "to speculate on Spanish vices, and its politics has consisted in taking advantage of them for its own convenience" (ibid.). Ortega ended his article with the ringing statement, borrowed from Cato, "Spaniards, your State does not exist! Reconstruct it! *Delenda est Monarchia!*" (XI, 279). He had used the phrase in two articles in the previous week, and it served as a useful rallying cry in the efforts of the intellectuals to establish a Republic. [1]

In February 1931 the government called for municipal elections, preparatory to general parliamentary elections. In the same month, Ortega, together with the distinguished physician and writer Gregorio Marañón and the novelist and poet Ramón Pérez de Ayala, published the manifesto of the "Agrupación al Servicio de la República" [Group at the Service of the Republic], calling for an association of intellectuals and professionals, dedicated to the implementation of the goals that Ortega had been enunciating since the days of the League for Political Education. Ortega's vision and style provided the inspiration and guidance for the Group as it asked for a government with the will to set for Spain goals that would unite all classes and regions in the creation of a common national future. Although the manifesto accused the monarchy of representing the interests of only the parasitic groups that benefitted from it, and living apart from the needs and aspirations of the nation, Ortega pointed out elsewhere in his own name that, because of their passivity, the Spanish people had to be held ultimately responsible. His group proposed to set a course between the "dead ends" of Bolshevism and Fascism, with a Republic "that will awaken in all Spaniards both dynamism and discipline, summoning them to the sovereign undertaking of resuscitating the history of Spain, renewing peninsular life in all its dimensions, attracting all skills, imposing an order of clean and energetic law, giving full transparency to justice, demanding much of every citizen: work, skill, efficiency, seriousness and the determination to raise our country fully to the level of the times" (XI, 126–27; 1931).

Despite the limitations imposed by censorship, the Group received considerable support from throughout the country in a short period of time.[2] Its platform included a recognition of the need to protect the dignity of all workers; the equal division of authority between a unicameral Parliament and the government; maximum authority for ten regions and a rejection of federalism; extensive use of technical commissions to make expert recommendations directly to Parliament; an increasingly controlled economy that would permit the modernization of the country in such urgent aspects as irrigation and electrification; the absolute separation of Church and state, to be achieved gradually over a period of ten years; and a balanced budget followed by a vigorous program of capital investment.

Not legally recognized until after the elections, the Group's participation in the campaign was limited, and in general it supported the Socialist Republican candidates. To the surprise of most people, Republican candidates received three times as many votes as the Monarchists. As Ortega later commented, "King Alfonso was too concerned about appearing clever and forgot to remain loyal in his personal relations to individuals and groups. The Spanish people vanquished him in a man-to-man combat."[3] The rapid abdication of the king and the declaration of the Republic on April 14, 1931, caught even the most fervent Republicans by surprise. From the beginning, Ortega was impressed by the smooth transition to the Republic, which he considered a mere change of form, but one that would necessitate a new life-style, both public and private. Since "Spain is an abnormally nonrevolutionary country,"[4] and Spanish history did not contain many examples of popular opposition to any regime, the Republic was truly a collective creation of the people and proof that a historical process was completing itself: "Spain always lived divided between two irreconcilable interests, the needs of the nation and the needs of the monarchy,"[5] and for more than a century, the monarchy had been losing ground.

Thirteen members of the Group at the Service of the Republic, including the three leaders, were elected in the parliamentary elections in June. In fact, the new Constituent Parliament contained so many distinguished figures that it was possible to speak of "the Republic of Intellectuals." Their idealism proved to be both the glory and the bane of the new politics, for their eloquence and prestige served to increase popular hopes, yet they were also the citizens most quickly frustrated by the various governments' constant inability to rise above factious squabbling. As a result, the next several years were a period of increasing disillusionment marked by the gradual withdrawal from politics of nearly all the liberal intellectuals, of whom the most notable were perhaps Unamuno and Ortega.

Central to the Group's vision was the strengthening of the position of the provinces within a new state. However, the new Constitution gave special recognition to the aspirations only of the Basque provinces and Catalonia, thus creating a division, in Ortega's opinion, into two Spains: one that was prickly and showed a desire to live apart, and one that was docile to the central authority. This, he warned, could serve only to inspire new local nationalisms where they had not previously existed, and failed to do anything whatever for the local life of the greater part of the country. He continued to advocate regional autonomy over the creation of a federalist state because it represented the bestowal by a strong government of specific powers upon regional governments, whereas federalism meant that sovereignty rested with the regions who could then surrender portions of it to the central government.

Under the monarchy, power had rested with the aristocracy, the rich conservative class, the army and the Church, but Ortega believed that only the army was treated with dignity and respect by the new regime. The conservative class, he admitted, was delinquent in neither helping to correct the abuses of the monarchy nor supporting the positive reforms that were enacted by the Republic. Moreover, the capitalists were irresponsible in immediately withdrawing from the country so much of their money before the new regime had a chance to consolidate itself. However, the government also displayed a hostile attitude toward the capitalists. Sincerely committed to the improvement of the lot of Spanish workers, Ortega felt that this could be achieved only by increasing the total wealth of the country. Consequently, he called for an "organized economy" and a National Economic Council that would consist of both Spanish and foreign experts who would investigate the plight of the national economy and report their findings directly to Parliament. Although he abhorred statism that could crush the individual, he favored a strong state that could intervene decisively in national life and shield the individual from abuse and exploitation by large financial interests.

The institution that had flourished under the monarchy and was most harshly treated by the Republic was, of course, the Church. While he tended to agree with Azaña's conviction that Spain was no longer truly Catholic,[6] he saw only unnecessary hostility in the Republic's suppression of Church schools and religious displays, and the stern restrictions on religious orders. The Church-state relationship was a part of Spanish tradition that should have been dissolved gradually and graciously in order to avoid unnecessary fears. The rapidity and apparent brutality of governmental policies merely served to create sympathy for the Church, and the mindless destruction of Church property by extremists exaggerated the Church's importance in contemporary Spanish life.

The Republic, he concluded, and the country at large, had arrived unprepared at this historic crossroads. Everyone agreed that the outstanding leaders were still lacking, but as Ortega said: "What did you want, Spaniards? That there should be waiting there, fully armed, marvelous men to govern you? But what had you done before to have those men?" (XI, 258; 1933). Decades of political and social inertia could not be swept aside in a matter of months. The Republic was the form of government demanded by the times because it could rise above special interests and put the best people in the positions where they could make their full contribution, but Spanish politics could simply not free itself of its legacy, which had been to reduce the imaginative scope of the nation.

Because the Republican governments revealed a continuation of the tendency to cater to special interests, Ortega feared that popular confusion would assume that the inadequacy of the politicians proved that the Republic itself was an error. There was an exaggerated predisposition for the Republic to look towards the past: first in a misguided desire to imitate previous republics,[7] instead of adapting the form to contemporary needs and using history to learn what should be avoided; and second, in a mean-spirited attempt to punish those who had previously ruled Spanish life. The tone tended to be

one of opposition rather than of affirmation, and after only five
months Ortega was moved to declare of the evolving Republic: "This
isn't it, this isn't it!" (XI, 387). In December 1931 he called a public
meeting to plead for a "rectification of the Republic," but many
believed that he had merely drifted to the Right.[8] With considerable
bitterness, Ortega himself later observed that "neither public opinion nor political groups paid me the slightest heed. This perfect and
total failure gives me the right to at least temporary silence" (XI, 520;
1933). In August 1932 he withdrew from politics and in October the
Group at the Service of the Republic was dissolved. After a long
silence, in December 1933 Ortega wrote an article ringingly entitled
"¡Viva la República!" in which he reasserted his republicanism, but
he never returned to the political arena. As Howard Lee Nostrand
commented: "Ortega was undeniably skillful as a political figure, yet
in that career his propensity for instructing people made him quite
unable either to compromise suavely with his opponents or to let
himself be led expediently by his followers."[9]

II   *The Definition of Human Life*

The period 1930 to 1936 was one of transition in Ortega's philosophy. The growing importance of existentialism stood between him
and his earlier biologism, and as a result he felt himself obliged to
refine his theory of vital reason. As his own life demonstrates, he was
more concerned than ever before about the problems of individual
authenticity, one's response to his vocation, what one could and
should do with his life, and, as always, what human life in fact is.
Repeated assaults on these problems led him to an increased awareness of historicity as a uniquely human element. Life is stretched
between its past, everything that has happened to it, everything that
it has been, no longer is, and can never be again, and its future, which
is created constantly in the light of an understanding of that experience. It is a ceaseless becoming as man is seen not as possessing an
unchanging nature, like other animals and things, but a history, and
Ortega's philosophy in those tumultuous years gradually evolved into
a closely defined concept of "historical reason," as human life was
described as a tissue of situations, an endless series of actions intended to give man the freedom to be himself, in total authenticity.
    In *Unas lecciones de metafísica* [Some Lessons in Metaphysics],
the skeleton of a university course given in the autumn of 1932,

Ortega set himself the task of returning to the very foundation of philosophy in order "to draw the permanent structure of life, what it always is."[10] He offered a series of succinct definitions: "*Life is what we do and what happens to us*" (40); it is drama, narration, "pure actuality" (41), in that while man lives *for* the future and *from* the past, he does so *in* the present. It is awareness within a constant becoming, "the ceaseless discovery that we make of ourselves and the world around us" (42); a continuous dialogue and interaction with everything that is not us, the other, our circumstance. We find ourselves thrust, without our consent, into a world that is uniquely our own but which we cannot choose and with which we must come to terms. Since its elements resist man and force him to look for solutions (114n, 118), life is a constant interpretation and justification of itself (137). Our life and our world are simultaneous and constitute our being. Faced with many possibilities and lost among them, we must attempt to determine our future, what we shall be. Human life is thus preoccupation (105).

Each human life is unique, and the drama lies in the fact that each life exists outside of one, perpetually dedicated to and dealing with the other that is the circumstance. In consequence, "Man is, in essence, a stranger, an émigré, an exile" (75). Ortega's growing proximity to some aspects of existentialism became clear as he stated: "Existence *sensu stricto* means, then, to be executively something, to be effectively what is; in short, execution of an essence" (78). Man makes his own essence constantly, but outside himself, in all that is not his essence. Life precedes all thought and conceptualizing regarding it; the self is merely one of its ingredients and secondary to it. Life depends on but is not body and soul, which are mere intellectualizations of things that are later, derivative hypotheses. Such concepts are things that we take for granted as we live and although their failure or absence would draw our attention to them, Ortega considered them "preevident" (58). Were we to convert them into direct consciousness, we would not be living them, but making of them one element that precedes another. Our life is made up only of such things as we are aware of, elements that we count on but that we may not know: "everything that makes up my life is manifest, patent; if not, I do not live it" (111). Each thing in my life is first a repertory of opportunities and obstacles that I take for granted: "when they are lacking they begin to have a being. Apparently, being is what is missing in our life, the enormous gap or void that thought, in its ceaseless effort, strives to fill" (101). I am insofar as I deal with the things of my circumstance, a fact that provokes confusion and disorientation, and makes metaphysics an inescapable part of the life of every man. It is the means by which he makes the decisions for his future, not as acquired secondhand, but as a response to an authentic need, and from it derive all his other actions. His thinking the things that are in his world, his interpreting them, is a creative act that gives rise to a less confusing world: "Metaphysics is not a science; it is the construction of the World, and that, constructing a world out of circumstances, is human life" (142). Thought is a secondary reality that is man's response to the threat of annihilation posed by things.

Man's search for an adequate solution to the conundrum can take either of two forms. Since his immediate and most natural tendency is to look for the answer in the stock offered by culture, he may allow his social self to dominate. This is the path of tradition and of "fictitious orientation." On the other hand, if man seriously examines such a solution, he may make it authentic by recreating it on the basis of his personal evidence. This is the path of reason and "authentic orientation." Life is, then, an endless search for individual vital truth; the truth that will provide a coherent system of interrelated certitudes that will explain what there is and make clear the ultimate truth that underlies them. The world is the totality of these things plus their reality plus me. Contrary to the conformist affirmations of realism, I am not another thing, for I cannot live apart; and contrary to the revolutionary affirmations of idealism, the world is not contained in me and externalized by my thinking about it. Yet, neither my world and all it contains, including me, can be without me, nor can I be without it. The unifying, vivifying ingredient is human life: "Reality is my coexistence with the thing" (173); "Truth is the pure coexistence of an 'I' with things, of some things in the presence of the 'I'" (174). There is no reality in the absence of a conscious human life.

In April 1932 Ortega published "Pidiendo un Goethe desde dentro" [Requesting a Goethe from Within], in which he suggested how his ideas of vital reason, vocation and destiny might be applied to biography. As he stated elsewhere, "The reality of life consists, then, not in what it is for him who sees it from without, but in what it is for him who is it from within, for him who is living it and in the measure that he lives it" (V, 30–31; 1933). In every life there is a destiny for which the individual is born; as part of his circumstance it precedes concepts and ideas regarding it. By means of his will, a man may choose or not to fulfill this vital project, but "he cannot correct it, change it, dispense with it or substitute it" (IV, 400). The drama that is life lies in the individual's struggle with his circumstance to fulfill or avoid his destiny. Biography, then, should attempt to answer two questions: first, what is the "vital vocation" of the subject, and second, in what measure was he faithful to that vocation, to what extent was his life authentic?[11]

The example of a man like Goethe, however, poses special problems, for his monumentality had led biographers to see him only from outside. Ortega requested that the principles of vital reason be applied so that Goethe could be seen from within the confines of his vital horizon. The irony of Goethe's life is that he was the first person to perceive that a life can be effectively seen only from the viewpoint of its own dramatic reality, yet after his decision to move to Weimar, he did little else but concern himself with his own life as a thing, at the expense of living it. His youth was truly romantic, full of vital struggle and thus the period of his most authentic works, when his vocation was still clear: "He had sprung up upon the planet with the mission of being a German writer charged with revolutionizing the literature of his country and, through his country, that of the world" (IV, 441). The end of youth is precisely that moment when the difficulties presented by the world set man at the decisive crossroads from the rest of his life, when he must choose, but Goethe was saved from that decision and immersed in a sort of eternal youth. When he accepted the invitation of Carl Augustus, he fled from his vocation and took refuge from any struggle to be, to realize himself fully. He chose to remain perpetually available for anything that life might offer and was, as a consequence, nothing fully. He lived from his ideas about life; the reality of his life was replaced by symbolism. Goethe's example touched Ortega deeply at a period in his own life when similar accusations could be made about him.[12]

III *Human Life in History*

The purpose of Ortega's 1933 university course that makes up *En torno a Galileo* (translated as *Man and Crisis*) was to apply scientifically his concept of generations to the period which, in his opinion, represented the turning point from which sprang the "Modern Age." As the culmination of ideas that had been repeatedly raised over the last fifteen years, the book enjoys a quality of completeness largely denied his other works.

Facts are merely part of life, and have no meaning outside a vital system. Historiography's first task, then, if any period is to be understood, is to determine the enduring general structure of life itself as well as those "ultimate certainties" about which man is intimately sure in any period. Individual life is determined and given structure by two preexisting features: "the thought of the times," which one may either accept or refute in order to deal with the spiritual difficulties that confront him; and the mechanical skills and techniques by means of which he may reduce life's material worries. Everything man does is a function of his concept of the world which he thereby constructs: "We shall say, then, that the world is the instrument *par excellence* that man produces, and that producing it is one and the same thing as his life, his being. Man is a born fabricator of universes" (V, 33). Such is the moving impulse of history, the reconstruction of which is historiography, intended to determine the changes that have taken place in the vital structure itself.

The postmodern period that was beginning displayed signs of the crumbling of some of the fundamental certainties of the previous age. When such alterations affect an entire generation, it is possible to speak of significant historical change, crisis. Thus, the generation, which Ortega defined as that group of people having approximately the same age and sharing a similar world, becomes the fundamental unit of historical measurement.[13] The coevality at any given time of three or more distinct generations provides history with its dynamism through what he called "the essential anachronism of history" (V, 38). Each generation both argues and collaborates with those preceding and following it; each is both a continuation and a source. Such a concept, Ortega believed, makes it possible to examine any age biographically, from within, by means of a "historical exactitude" that goes beyond mere dates of birth. He preferred to speak of a "zone of dates" as a basis for dividing a man's life into five stages, which "are of our life and not, primarily, of our organisms" (V, 47). These are periods of approximately fifteen years each: childhood, when one attempts to come to grips with one's circumstance; youth, which is mainly devoted to the mastery of things; initiation, the period from thirty to forty-five that is filled with tension as one prepares to enter upon the historical stage; dominance, the period from forty-five to sixty that is the time of vital fulfillment, power, and influence; and old age, the period from sixty to seventy-five, when one becomes an impartial representative of and authority on the previous way of being. The real movement of history, however, is effected by the two generations who coexist between thirty and sixty: those who are preparing to rule and those who hold power.

The application of this concept to historical rhythms required that Ortega isolate the "decisive generation" for the Modern Age and, within it, the decisive figure. Not surprisingly, he chose Descartes, who reached the age of thirty in 1626, a year that served to establish the key dates of the preceding generations in order to trace back the stages of the crisis that was resolved by Descartes's generation. Ortega found that between 1350 and 1550 man ceased to hold to the beliefs of Christianity, a system that had been secure for the preceding age, and began to try to prepare himself for new beliefs. The fifteenth century was the center of the crisis: the transitional, unstable moment in which both medieval life and the new life coexisted in an uneasy and dynamic duality that was part of fifteenth-century man, suspended between an inert faith in the supernatural and a vibrant faith in himself. The Spanish humanist Juan Vives (1492–1540) symbolized this.[14]

A new element, the history of having previously been Christian, became an integral part of European man. The Christian experience had left the lesson that life must be dedicated to something; it must have a mission and a responsibility. This awareness continued to shape human life up to the end of the nineteenth century as various efforts were made "to fill the space in the European soul that the evaporation of Christianity had left empty" (V, 156). The antithetical generations that lived through the conflicting systems of belief were those that gradually brought clarity out of confusion. Galileo (1564–1642) was invoked as the pivotal figure who had been forced by an antiquated cosmovision to renounce the very theory that was to give rise to the development of modern physics, the cornerstone of the Modern Age. He symbolized the Renaissance, an age of profound change in which he and his generation revolutionized man's vital horizon and established the beliefs of a period that, three centuries later, was drawing to a close. He showed the way for modern science by combining facts with an imagined reality in such a way as to bring them into complete harmony, and contributed to make of science "the faith by which modern European man lives" (V, 34). The crisis lasted until 1650, when Descartes had written his works and the creation of modern man was complete. This was the beginning of the period of culmination of the Modern Age that lasted until the first Romantic generation, that of Goethe, Goya, and Mirabeau. Man had created a new world as he had moved from a belief that God is truth to a belief that science is truth, a belief that truth resides in human reason.

Whenever culture, which is the stock of solutions, the interpretative order that man imposes on the chaos surrounding him, can be taken for granted, it loses its vitality. It ceases to affect man until it leaves him alienated and defenseless once more. He may avoid the problem by contenting himself with ready-made formulae inherited from previous generations, but such a process, if unchecked, can lead to spiritual inertia as individual initiative is replaced by collective attitudes, unquestioningly adopted. In times of crisis, man's task is to create new vital beliefs by withdrawing into the intimacy that he alone of the animals has. Ortega thus seriously questioned the two traditional assumptions of philosophy: that everything has a being that is hidden from man, and that it is natural that man should strive to discover and define this being. Rather, he argued, intelligence is a tool of life: man needs to know only what he can depend on in those things that surround and affect him. Therefore, he must construct an intellectual system in which he can truly believe.

Like those of other animals, man's efforts are all, to some extent, directed at sustaining life, but his will and his intellect also endow him with the ability to create things that do not already exist in nature, in his circumstance. This repertory of secondary activities is technology, which can alleviate the primary needs by slightly altering man's circumstance and reducing the urgency of its demands upon him. In "Meditación de la técnica" [Meditation on Technology, 1933] Ortega examined the meaning of technology for man's relationship with his world, in contrast with the vital beliefs that were collectively held. Technology is man's unique grip on his circumstance, an alteration of his world: "it is the adaptation of the medium to the subject" (V, 326), a possibility not open to other animals. Man's capacity for setting aside momentarily the primary activities allows him to attend to his intimacy, his subjective needs. Human life, then, is less a question of being than of well-being; man's aspirations are satisfied only in what goes beyond mere biological necessity. In short, "for man, only the objectively superfluous is necessary" (V, 328), for he does not truly feel the biological demands.

Technology is historically relative as it serves to satisfy ever-changing, uniquely human needs. As a bulwark against vital insecurity, it is an activity undertaken by each man in view of the ease or difficulty he finds in his circumstance as he creates himself towards the realization of his vital project. He cannot be a man without technology, for it is the mechanical fact that increases his freedom to be and become himself, to insert himself in the world. Technology in no way defines what man must become, but it is an instrument of his will that alters his vital horizon and follows from his awareness of his authentic desires. Without an authentically felt vital program to fulfill, technology flounders.

Ortega distinguished three stages in technological evolution. The first was the age of technological innovation as the result of chance, a spontaneous creation of a primitive mind that, because it did not invent it in order to solve any specific problem, could not recognize its full possibilities. The scarcity of such creations in a primitive world made technology all but indistinguishable from primary, more purely natural actions. Moreover, although it seemed like a new facet of nature that had magically manifested itself, its essential simplicity made it universally accessible. In this primitive stage, the creative consciousness is absent.

Neither does the second stage permit technology to be perceived as an independent order of activity, nor does it irrevocably separate man from a return to a more primitive style of life, yet its increased complexity causes it to be practiced primarily by artisans. Although the artisan is both inventor and worker, the consciousness of invention is still restricted by the perception of craftsmanship as submission to a tradition. As such, it is limited to the creation and refinement of tools that are extensions of man's own natural abilities. At this stage there exists a balance between nature and technology, as could be seen in medieval Europe. Only when man can be replaced by a machine, a mechanism that is more than an extension of him, do the technologist and the worker fulfill different functions as technology is seen as definitively apart and free from human limitations. In this third stage, man's perception of his limitations all but disappears. Simultaneously, it becomes impossible for man to live without technology as it interposes itself between him and nature. In contemporary Europe, the dramatic expansion of technology had facilitated the satisfaction of needs that man did not feel in his own intimacy. Technology no longer sprang from authentic individual vocations, but had become anonymous.

In contemporary Western society, Ortega saw that only a highly developed technology made it possible for a rapidly increased population to live well. The danger lay in the fact that it was also seen as a natural activity and had come to represent a jungle no less threatening than that faced by primitive man. The machine, once invented, is by definition automatic and dispenses with its creator, thus leaving only the worker. Since the Renaissance, man had gradually become subjugated to the machine and had lost his sense of the natural as technology lost its reference to life and became analytical, scientific, and methodical. The pure imagining of artifices, without a preconceived purpose, began the process by which the craftsman was replaced by the engineer for whom technology is everything, a parallel world in which man invents for the sake of inventing, certain of attaining the desired result. Although the battle of man against the material world appeared to have been won, Ortega warned that life is "also the battle of man with his soul" (V, 375), for which contemporary man was ill-prepared, lulled as he was by his technical proficiency and a stock of solutions for problems that he did not sense. [15]

Ortega gave a concrete example of such a process in "La misión del bibliotecario" [The Mission of the Librarian, 1935], in which he traced the evolution of the book from a personally felt vocation into a social necessity that demanded that the care and ordering of books become a profession. The political demands placed upon the book since the invention of printing had been made possible by technological advancement that he now called upon to bring the book back under man's control. Too many books had led people to read badly and accept the ideas of others without adequate reflection. The future of librarianship, he felt, lay in automation and in aiding the reader to select the material of most use from the torrent with which he was confronted. Too many books were being published that were not the result of a personal vocation, leading to "the fabrication of the false book" (V, 232), the book that offered only a fraction of a thought, torn out of the vital context that should have given it life. Technology must be employed to harness the forces that it had made possible.

IV *The Intellectualization of History*

In "Historia como sistema" [History as a System, 1935] Ortega began to develop the distinction between ideas as an intellectual product that man has, and beliefs, that man is. These latter, even when apparently contradictory, form a living pattern for his life, with an influence far more profound than that of ideas and a hierarchical scale that allows the historian to determine the "fundamental belief, the decisive one, the one that carries and gives life to all the others."

The Modern Age had been defined by a collective belief that reality was rational, like the human mind, and that there was a necessary correspondence between the two that reason could determine. This belief engendered a faith that was sufficient for man to live by, but the contemporary age, while still clinging to the shell of this belief, had ceased to have faith in it. The most immediate victim was physical and mathematical science, ruler of the modern hierarchy, which, although it had so successfully conquered the mysteries of nature, those things that simply are, was constitutionally unable to provide definitive answers to those ultimate questions touching on the dramatic character of life. Life's demand for truth now required other means.

The battle had begun to be waged in the *Geisteswissenschaften* of the nineteenth century,[16] in which was maintained, however, the traditional division between things that are and things that think. For Ortega, both had a "static consistency" and this method implied merely a shift of the stress from one sort of invariability to another. Reality was still intellectualized as it was perceived as possessing identity and corresponding to an invariable pattern. The idea of a human nature, he insisted, had to be superseded, as did the belief that the human spirit was a thing and, therefore, self-sufficient. It was time to look upon "human life as it is lived by each and every one" (VI, 32), something that is always happening, but never finished, "a gerundive and not a participle" (VI, 33), a combination of becoming (passive) and a way of becoming (active). Human life is "constitutive instability" (VI, 34), rich in imagination, creativity, and potentiality and thus lacking in absolute identity. No part of it is free from change.

Moreover, this inexorable movement that is human life is also determined by its past. On the level of society, this is no less true, but the effect of the accumulated past takes longer to bring about change. Although the presence of the past is the most nearly static element in human life, it is what life was and no longer is. Since the system of history forbids the understanding of any one stage without an understanding of the previous stages that it contains and that made it possible, an understanding of either individual or collective man can be achieved only through the narration that is historical reason. It alone can capture his mobility. "Man does not have a nature, but he does have . . . a history" (VI, 41), and he is its creator. So that he might learn to understand more authentically what he is, he must understand history: both his own and that of the collectivity to which he belongs. Historical reason was to become the new science; Ortega saw it as "literally, *what had happened to man, constituting substantive reason,* the revelation of a reality that transcends man's theories and that is he himself beneath his theories" (VI, 50).

"Ideas y creencias" [Ideas and Beliefs], begun in December 1934, provides a succinct analysis of the distinction that was tentatively explored in "History as a System" and continues to lay the bases for historical reason. Man has ideas that he may develop, examine, discuss, defend, and transmit, but he lives from his beliefs and is inseparable from them. The distinction lies not in the degree to which either is true, but rather in the force that they exert on a man's way of living. Ideas are intellectual constructions which are thought, whereas man takes beliefs for granted and assumes them in his other activities. His beliefs seem to precede him and are not apparently a result; they are the implicit and largely unconscious suppositions from which he sets out. Ideas, however, exist for him only when he directs his attention to thinking them, and he always has the choice whether to do so or not. Their existence depends on his will, whereas his beliefs are as inescapable as they are involuntary. Ideas may be subjected to proof and questioned, and their validity lies in the degree to which they fit in with other ideas in an intellectual combination. To some extent, then, they are imaginary and at one remove from man's intimate reality. It cannot be denied, however, that ideas may also succeed in becoming fundamental presuppositions that man comes to accept automatically, as can be seen in his modern belief in reason. Doubt, in which man may also find himself, is simply a negative belief, directed toward a reality that is ambiguous and unstable and which the imaginative power of ideas is called upon to attempt to resolve. Since the Renaissance, man's faith in reason had made it the ultimate arbiter of all such disputes.

Ortega considered man's unique intimacy to be "our imaginary world, the world of our ideas" (V, 401). It is unlike raw external reality in that it is clearer and less fraught with confusion and conflict, yet it is no less a part of man's total reality. From it derives his ability to interpret and return to his external reality. It is the realm of artificial constructions such as science and poetry and only this inner world can adhere to the laws of exactitude. Regardless of how closely it corresponds to the external world, man has no choice but to lead a double life, moving between one, which is his plan or interpretation, and the other, which is the object of such an effort. From the experience of doubting and testing, the errors of interpretation and the lack of correspondence, man comes closer to being right, but he must also understand his history so as to preserve the lesson of those errors.

CHAPTER 6

The Practice of Historical Reason

ORTEGA'S last two decades are the subject of no less controversy than the rest of his career. His disciple, José Gaos, considers it to be a period of declining originality, a time of disappointment and withdrawal. Others, however, see it as Ortega's finest hour as he was free at last to dedicate himself completely to pursuing his philosophical concerns in a more methodical way than had previously been possible.[1] For a decade, he lived in exile, largely ignored abroad and either forgotten or discredited in Spain, where his influence waned dramatically. He also suffered from deteriorating health and these circumstances cannot be discounted in considering the tone of pessimism, disappointment, and growing bitterness that was so often in evidence.

I   Historical Reason and the Nature of Thought

It was logical that five years of exile would aggravate Ortega's anxiety regarding the proper role of the intellectual enterprise in the contemporary world.[2] In late 1941, *Logos,* a journal of the University of Buenos Aires, published "Apuntes sobre el pensamiento. Su teurgia y su demiurgia" [Notes on Thought. Its Theurgy and Demiurgy], in which Ortega noted that in recent years not only had there been a reduction in the expectations of thought: "The fact is that Thought is not fashionable" (V, 519), but that this was a sign of a crisis even more dramatic than that which had occurred in the fifteenth century: "We know that something tremendous is happening to Thought, but we do not know what is happening to it and even less whether what is happening is good or bad" (V, 520). Consistent with the principles of historical reason, he attempted to demonstrate that thought is a vital activity, a primary reality that manifests itself in many different mental activities of which knowledge is but one mode, the child of reason, and as such, subject to historical alteration. Modern development had revealed that reason and knowledge no longer inspired the same faith as in the late nineteenth century, a discovery that had repercussions in all aspects of intellectual activity and man's perception as he confronted problems that reason had promised to solve.

Thought is the organization of mechanical mental actions in order to achieve a result, but it is constitutively unsatisfactory because that result is never adequately achieved. The nature of thought cannot be discovered by either psychology or logic for these succeed in revealing only partial truths while simultaneously concealing other truths, not the least of which is the fact that thought and knowledge are not necessarily one, or that while knowledge is indeed thought, the reverse need not be true. Ortega offered a first definition: "Thought is what we do—*whatever it may be*—in order to get out of the doubt into which we have fallen and to manage to be right again" (V, 530). Thought is a vital activity. Man *needs* to think, since life and the world are constantly unresolved problems for him, but the methods, the intellectual actions employed, are constructions that he makes, of which knowledge is but one that presupposes a fixed reality that can be captured by a disciplined mental effort. It is the result of previous processes and therefore not an example of all that thought is.

For the ancient Greeks the belief in knowledge had been supported by the conviction that things had a being beneath the surface that could be known, but such a belief had evaporated in the postmodern world, leaving defenseless the belief that the intellect could conquer things. Thus was changed the nature of thought; the world and life were once more seen as problematic. Reason and intelligence had largely succeeded in conquering material problems, but they were unable alone to resolve ethical dilemmas, and had in fact become part of the problem. Nevertheless, other paths remained open to thought and it fell to philosophy to explore them. Since philosophy is predicated upon thought, it is indispensable in some form to human life, whereas knowledge is not absolute, but "merely historical" (V, 533); it is only one possible mode of philosophy.

In "Origen y epílogo de la filosofía" [The Origin and Epilogue of Philosophy, 1943] Ortega repeated his conviction that the history of philosophy is fundamentally sequential, a continuous line of unsuccessful doctrines from which spring new attempts, each of which begins as a criticism of its predecessors and necessarily ends in partial failure, an insufficient truth caused by the fact that, since each idea leads dialectically to another, the process had been interrupted too soon. Succeeding attempts, like the history of mankind, absorb the past and continue to move toward completion.

Ortega also reaffirmed his conviction that knowledge is perspective in that man knows only a series of aspects of things, but cannot perceive or know all aspects at once. Thus, knowledge of a thing is necessarily sequential also, a dialectical interpretation in which one aspect implies the others. Ortega summarized the "articulations" of dialectical thought as stopping to look at each aspect of a thing, continuing to think while passing on to another, contiguous, aspect, and integrating these various aspects into a sufficiently complete whole (IX, 374–75). In some sense, this is rendered more complicated by the fact that basic to all philosophies is a tendency to divide the world into the aspect that can be seen and the aspect that is dialectically implied, with a connection that may be more or less close. Because it is always a new way of thinking, philosophy does not settle for the usual world. The free choice of principles to replace dead gods—a sort of atheism—is, claimed Ortega, the creation of philosophy, and he considered an important facet of serious thinkers to be their unwillingness to accept unquestioned the commonly held beliefs.

II *Art as the Historical Vanguard*

Repeatedly, Ortega declared that any major alteration in the way of thinking appeared first in the arts. Spain had produced outstanding examples of two critical moments in European thought in two of her greatest painters: Velázquez, who was a member of the generation in which the Modern Age became consolidated; and Goya, who belonged to the generation that made the transition towards the decline of the Modern Age. For more than a decade, Ortega returned to the enigma that was Velázquez through analysis, commentary, and the publication of contemporary texts, with the intention of giving substance to the first half of the Spanish seventeenth century. What was possibly the most important single generation in the history of the West included Calderón and Gracián in Spain; Claude Lorraine, Poussin, and Descartes in France; and Van Dyck in Flanders. Moreover, it included the generation that Ortega considered to be the entire history of Spanish painting before Goya: the four painters from Seville: Velázquez, Ribera, Zurbarán, and Alonso Cano.[3] Such a circumstance clearly transcends mere biography and demands the methods of historical reason. For this generation, painting was the form that had the greatest impact. It was, however, the moment of the last stage in the development of Italian painting, of which the Spanish artistic ambit was only the periphery where new developments were felt last and where its final style arose. Velázquez, in fact, completed an arc that had begun with Giotto, but Ortega's interest in Velázquez was due to the fact that, alone among his Spanish contemporaries, he went against the current of his times, not in a spirit of rebellion, but merely of independence.

Painting begins where language and poetry leave off and, because of its muteness, always demands interpretation. Ortega called it "the most hermetic of the arts" (VII, 491), and found it ceaselessly dynamic because it is constitutionally inexhaustible. Interpretation, however, is necessarily historic, for the painter is always present and it is incumbent upon the viewer to attempt to understand what painting meant for him, what moved him to paint, what dictated his style, and what were the presuppositions from which he worked. In Velázquez's time, painting had acquired a vital role in Spain, and especially in Seville, and large segments of that society understood it to such an extent that the experimental character of his work could interest them.

Every painting is a dynamic tension between what the objects depicted are and the style that is imposed upon them: "Art is not the thing as it is outside the picture, but the style that is imprinted upon it in the picture" (VIII, 586). The balance between these forces gives the picture its magical power to transform things, to free them a bit from the limits of what they are, and to allow them to be something slightly different. The natural evolution in art and all human forms is toward ever more stylization until art itself becomes suffocated by formalism. Velázquez, however, went against the current of his times and absented himself from his paintings, avoiding all excesses of mannerism and confession in order to leave the viewer alone with the objects. He separated painting from sculpture and the rules of form and schematized the reality of his subjects into a "pure vocabulary of color" (VIII, 612). He made painting into its own norm and created Spanish painting, based on the primacy of purely pictorial values. His very idea of what painting was sprang from his unique way of being: he turned his back on his public and devoted himself to the solution of problems. Despite its appearance of calm and ease, his work was the result of a sustained effort and a severe discipline, and it contains the energy and struggle that are absent from his anecdotal biography.

Ortega discarded as unimportant all but one of the known facts of Velázquez's life, and laid stress only upon his appointment as court painter to Philip IV. At this moment, the pattern for the rest of his life was established. Despite his technical facility and the great amount of free time at his disposal, he painted relatively little, a fact that led Ortega to suspect him of indolence, an indication that he was, in fact, "one of the men who in a most exemplary way has known how . . . not to exist" (VIII, 462). His personal and artistic independence was total, and Ortega found that the secret of Velázquez was that "he does not want, he has never wanted, to be a painter" (VIII, 466). Rather, his ambition was to be a nobleman, and chance had facilitated his entry into the Court where he could feel that he was the nobleman that he sensed he must be. Painting occupied only a small corner of his life and each work represented not self-expression, but the solution of a problem that, once conquered, he needed not consider again. Nevertheless, from the time of his arrival in Madrid, all his works were of an equal, high quality. His cool detachment rendered his treatment exceptionally objective, an attitude that was in itself revolutionary in that it lent dignity to a technique that was, at the time, considered inartistic because it rested on naturalness, the uncompromisingly commonplace, and made of the painter a mere instrument. This was Velázquez's "realism."

Ortega laid much importance by the necessary "derealization" carried out by all works of art. Velázquez effected a revolution by causing real, everyday objects to take on all the artistic prestige of the unreal and the imaginary that were still the nucleus of artistic attention. In his hands, the most banal subject matter became surprising as he stripped objects down and eliminated their tactile quality. He painted only the elements that presented themselves to the eye, "reality as appearance" (VIII, 478), the object as it eternally comes into being in the eye of the viewer, as light and color, not as touch and form. There is added no apparent interpretation of the subject matter, but rather an interest limited to the mere presence of the objects, undeformed by any human idealization that gives them a convenient preciseness that they otherwise lack.

No less significant was his choice of themes. Because he believed that aesthetic emotion could be produced in ways other than the depiction of fantasies, his artistic world virtually never went beyond the limits of the known world. Alone among contemporary painters, "he senses a satiety of beauty and poetry, and a longing for prose" (VIII, 483). The abstract ideal of Beauty, the essential deformation implied by "what things would be if they were as we want them" (VIII, 574), characteristic of the Italian tradition, was banished as he returned to the "real object." Unlike his Baroque contemporaries, Velázquez painted not the synthesis of a series of movements, but a moment in the existence of his subjects, an instant rendered eternal. His independence and ultimate influence in painting were no less dramatic than those of Descartes in philosophy, for in both cases reality was allowed to appear as it is, unadorned, prosaic, and pure.

Ortega began his 1948 study of Goya with words similar to those that he applied to Goethe: "Goya is a fact of the first order, belonging to the destiny of the West" (VII, 505). Like his contemporaries Mirabeau and Goethe, he was the sharp edge between two ages and his work showed the continuation of the traditions of the past while representing a great and unexpected leap into the future. He offered a useful complement to Goethe in Ortega's analyses, for he knew instinctively, although not intellectually, from a very early age what he had to be and his life, seen from within, is a slow movement toward vital fulfillment. Rude and untutored, the rustic from Aragón moved gradually and inexorably to become the first painter of Spain and possibly of Europe. The pattern of his development reveals that, like Mirabeau, he carried this destiny within him in everything that he did.

The Goya that had to be emerged because of two important facts. First, in 1775, the same year Goethe settled in Weimar, Goya left Zaragoza for Madrid where he was first exposed to the atmosphere of the Royal Palace that was an essential stimulus in his evolution both as an artist and as a man. A decade later, his social setting expanded once more as he came into close contact with the nobility and the intellectuals of the Spanish Enlightenment. This experience awoke in him new possibilities as he irrevocably left the traditional world of the Spanish peasant and became part of his historical generation. Both these changes in Goya's vital horizon occurred at moments when his development required them, and he incorporated them into his evolution, but neither of them removed from him his past. Ortega observed that while Goya was possessed by his painting, he always saw himself, in accordance with the accepted social standing of Spanish painters for a century, as a craftsman, immensely proud of all his technical skills, and such Romantic conceits as genius and inspiration played no part in his vision of himself. He remained "a great stammering painter" (VII, 521) who, while never truly close to the themes and subjects of his works, was intimately bound up with the paintings themselves. He carried deep within himself mysterious powers that were transferred to his art, and with him, Romanticism appeared for the first time in painting.

His contact with the aristocracy and the intelligentsia did not occur until Goya was nearly forty, when his being demanded the attitudes of people who controlled their spontaneous impulses and molded themselves to certain ideals. While Goethe agonized over and avoided his destiny, Goya instinctively allowed his to become firm. His art showed an ever greater tendency toward aristocratic selectivity, a fact that was undoubtedly at odds with his rusticity; Ortega spoke of "a popular soul with a confused awareness of sublime norms" (VII, 536). Nonetheless, this dynamism led toward his fulfillment as a painter as, by being torn away from tradition and by rejecting pure spontaneity, he penetrated to "more reflexive and deeper zones of his being" (ibid.). Goya's fulfillment is, in large measure, the result of these inner contradictions which always leave the viewer unresolved. Nonetheless, his sense of self coincided totally with his profession as a painter and he was always what he felt he had to be. As Ortega said, "This is a deformed genius who drags himself along crippled and, leaning precisely on his own awkwardness, manages to make the most agile leaps towards the peak of art" (VII, 558), and he summed up his analysis with the observation that "Goya is an extreme example of the human situation that we may call 'the creative man'" (VII, 562).[4]

III   *The Diversion of Theater*

Two contemporaneous texts represented a return by Ortega to certain aspects of his interest in the sportive nature of life and the need for apparently superfluous activities. "Idea del teatro" [The Idea of the Theater] was a lecture delivered in Lisbon on April 13, 1946, and repeated on May 4 when Ortega returned to Spain after almost a decade in exile, as a guest at the ceremonies marking the reopening of the Madrid Ateneo. In an appendix to the published text of the lecture, entitled "Máscaras" [Masks], he applied the methods of historical reason to the very origins of the theater, in the collective character of Greek religion, from which sprang public ceremonies, festivals, and spectacles that were, in their origin, an integral part of religious expression and, as such, filled an authentic vital need.

The festivals dedicated to the cult of Dionysus in particular took on a markedly dramatic character and became an important occasion for enthusiastic escape from the daily routine by providing a sort of "ultralife" (VII, 480) that gave the sensation of living in another existence. The manic, passionate, festive, and often deliberately contradictory nature of Dionysus and his cult pointed toward a life that was truly divine in character: "Surrender to Dionysus and the transcendent reality that he symbolizes is alienation, ecstatic madness—'mania'" (VII, 483). It was here that Ortega found the "pre-theater" (VII, 486). Religion and festival were as one, and the masking of the figure of Bacchus during the Roman Empire further helped man to be other than he was in daily life, to feel himself more powerful. This eternal awareness of the discrepancy between what he is and what he feels he should be has always driven man to live metaphorically, in a state of "almost being" something else, and the theater is the vital response, on the part of both audience and actors, to eliminate that discrepancy and give poetry to life. Like pre-Christian religion, it provides another world to which man can escape; like sports and games, it provides a suspension of life.[5]

In "The Idea of the Theater," Ortega considered the way this vital function is revealed in the modern theater's physical construction. First, it is a building that separates an inner space from the everyday world.[6] Inside it consists of a series of three essential dualities. There is the architecture that divides the building into a section for the actors and another for the audience, separated by a proscenium arch that symbolizes both the division and the dynamic relationship that must exist between them. Thus arises the human duality, between activity and passivity. The furnishings demonstrate that the public is expected to remain still and attentive, while the actors, in their open space, are to be active but with the public in mind. The third duality is functional: one group is there to see and the other to be seen. The literary element is secondary to the purely visual and Ortega's concern was directed towards the theater as a human activity.

Like the mask of the Bacchic orgy, the spectacle is pure metaphor in which the actor creates another being that subsumes his own: "So that what is *not* real, the unreal . . . has the strength, the magical power, to cause the real to disappear" (VII, 458). The materiality of the actors induces the viewer to forget who he "really" is. The essential character of the theater is phantasmagoric, and both the public and the actors must be sufficiently alert to retain their "sense of unreality" (VII, 464),[7] so as to enter consciously the alternative world of fiction, farce, and fantasy.

IV *The Return to Leibniz*

The major result of Ortega's stay in Lisbon was *La idea de principio en Leibniz y la evolución de la teoría deductiva* [The Idea of Principle in Leibniz and the Evolution of Deductive Theory, 1947], his longest and most uncompromising work.[8] The book was never finished, and ends on the very threshold of the problem announced in the first half of the working title: to reexamine according to his own philosophy the thought of one of the most important inspirations of the neo-Kantianism of Marburg. Moved once more by the crisis of principles in the physical sciences, Ortega took the principle as the basis for examining the philosophic pattern established by Aristotle and leading through the Stoics and Scholasticism up to Descartes and the beginning of modern thought. He set out from his conviction that philosophy is not, like other sciences, merely based on organizing principles that serve to explain, but has as its aim the very discovery of ultimate or radical principles.

To Ortega it seemed axiomatic that a principle is the one thing that cannot be further broken down, for it is the source of everything else. "The essential character of a principle is, then, that something follows it, and not that nothing precedes it" (VIII, 66), a characteristic that makes it valid within both the finite and the infinite orders. By working our way backward in logic we can reach certain principles that are truly independent and that give truth to their consequences. Emerging from these radical principles, however, every other element is both a consequence (of a principle) and a "relative principle" (for a further consequence). As such it provides the truth of its consequence, but as Ortega noted, it thereby makes truth itself ambiguous. On the one hand, truth is then a result and as such, reasonable, although in the case of radical principles, unprovable and necessarily unproven; it is self-evident and thus irrational. On the other hand, the conclusion could be that radical principles are not in fact true in themselves, but are merely stipulated in order to produce the truth of their consequences, the relative principles. The preference for one approach or the other serves to reveal the two different ways of thinking that are pre- and post-Cartesian thought.

Methods of thought for the exact sciences are predicated upon logicality, but their relationship to external reality is tenuous, for logical operations can be performed only on concepts. For all cognition, the concept was still the keystone for Ortega, who considered it to be the prelogical interpretation, the definition of the intuition of a thing. Herein lies the tension of the history of thought that has tried to identify things with concepts in such a way that the apparent exactness of thought has tended to ignore those aspects of things that do not conform to the concept. Plato had shown that definition, a reduction into basic elements, is the supreme form of reason, and Aristotle and Scholasticism started their deductive process from the definition. Until Descartes, definition was considered to be analytical, but it was a reduction not achieved by logical means, for while the definition gives names to the components, these are not defined but intuited. Thus defining is a process of both analysis and synthesis, an adding to intuition: "The definition is the formula that makes analytically explicit the intuitive knowledge of what a thing is, a knowledge that, implicitly, I already had" (VIII, 114). Nonetheless, the resulting elements are the material from which logical operations must start. For the moderns, however, definition would become the last step in the cognitive process.

Ortega found an illogical duality in pre-Cartesian notions of truth because the methods of proving were secondary forms of thinking that derived from "evidencing," which is assumed, irrational, but which reaches the primary propositions. Aristotle insisted that scientific thinking must start out from *principiae maximae* that, although unprovable, are true, but with Descartes a radical alteration took place: "The ancients thought *from* Being, whereas the moderns, beginning with Descartes, think from thinking, from 'ideas'" (VIII, 142). Parmenides had seen "Reality as Reality only when and insofar as it coincides with concepts" (VIII, 210), because he thought that logical thinking was the projection of reality over the human mind, and while Aristotle was certainly heir to Eleatic logicality, for him, principles were sensual; being manifests itself in the senses. To the modern mind, such "sense-perceptible intuition" (VIII, 142)[9] created an overabundance of principles. The Moderns could not accept this belief that the senses are knowledge, and believed rather that knowledge is subsequent. Modern philosophy found that "the defect in the traditional method is . . . the excessive and inappropriate importance that it grants to experience. This experience is what obliges us to call it empiricism in a pejorative sense" (VIII, 183).

Aristotle's principles, the result of empirical deduction, led only to practical truths, truth as a working assumption. On the one hand, the principle was a proposition that had its own class of truth, evidentiary, not dependent on proof, whereas on the other, it must lead to and provide the basis for a series of other truths. It was both "a true isolated and independent proposition," and also "a principle of demonstration and, hence, inseparable from the propositions which are its consequences" (VIII, 207). For Aristotle, the principle was above all "that proposition from which reasoning sets out" (VIII, 189), and could be merely plausible. It was provisional and sufficient; its main characteristic was to be first, whereas for modern thought, greater importance was given to subsequence.

Until Descartes, European thought lived in the shadow of Aristotle. The Stoics believed that principles emerged spontaneously and were not the product of intelligence but of common opinion and "blind assumption through collective suggestion" (VIII, 249). Since man is a product of Nature, they were material. In the late Middle Ages, Scholasticism functioned as the heir of Aristotle, a method of interpretation devoting assiduous attention to his philosophy, but without being able to understand the assumptions and authentic problems that had caused it to come into existence. By the sixteenth and seventeenth centuries, philosophy had come to see itself as only one form of knowledge, and was dominated by a mentality rooted in the methods of mathematics. However, by 1750, philosophy had begun to be more fundamentally influenced by the dramatically evolving methods of the physical sciences. Leibniz was the crucial figure, for while being one of the first to move towards the new orientation, he was no less the last representative of the previous attitude. In this light, Ortega placed him on a level with two predecessors, François Viète (1540–1603), creator of algebra, and Descartes, creator of analytical geometry.

Ortega believed that these were significant steps in the evolution of deductive reasoning for the next three and a half centuries. Algebra made possible a new way of thinking in which signs are used only as signs: the algebraic formula "serves us as both the name and the definition of the number. It names *by means of* the definition, which is the ideal of a name" (VIII, 95). Although the separation of algebra and geometry still existed, underlying both methods is a "basic intuition" (VIII, 97)—quantity and extension—that is not inherently logical or reducible, but self-evident. Out of this Descartes would create analytical geometry, predicated upon his realization that geometric and numerical relations could in fact be expressed in terms of each other. As a mathematical thinker, he also broke with the Aristotelian past by considering the sciences as one, as human knowledge. Ortega considered this declaration of "the communicability of the genera" to be the beginning of the true European Renaissance (VIII, 225).

Science was henceforth the totality of deductive reasoning. Contrary to Aristotle, Descartes relegated sense-perception to a rank secondary to rationality, the evidence of what he called "intuition," a clear understanding of connections, "that sets out from supposed truths and on the basis of them recognizes a new one" (VIII, 321). However, such intuition is a function of deduction, which moves from one truth to another by means of "the relationship of evident connection between each two truths" (ibid.). For Descartes, philosophy was rooted in its doubt of all human knowledge, without which there is no intellectual truth. For this reason, he considered arithmetic and geometry to be exemplary because they are the sure result of deductive reasoning and leave no room for doubt. The importance of mathematics and its function as "pure understanding" to both Descartes and Leibniz lay in its quality as an idea, a fantasy, that can always be more exact than our conception of reality itself, and which as a human creation, like poetry, and unlike beliefs, can be revoked or unmade. Descartes represented a new starting-point, a specific level of experience, in the evolution of philosophy. The cognitive power was seen as being homogeneous.[10]

V   *The Structure of Society in History*

Del Imperio Romano [On the Roman Empire], published in 1940 in *La Nación* of Buenos Aires, was translated into English as *Concord and Liberty*, a felicitous title that shows that Ortega once more failed to fulfill the promise of his original title. He had intended to examine the history of Rome as the model that it was: an entire civilization whose creation, culmination, and decay were completely documented and well known to contemporary man, and that offered parallels with contemporary Europe.[11] Cicero, like Ortega, had discerned in the crises of society "the very condition on which is founded and from which emerges the health of the State" (VI, 57), and his use of the terms *concordia* and *libertas* in *De re publica* appeared to offer the key to the lessons that might be derived from the history of the Empire. *Concordia* meant for Cicero the common agreement of a people on certain fundamental matters, the force that binds a state and underlies discord in less essential matters. When such basic agreement crumbles, however, the state and the community may be destroyed, confronting man with the sensation of a radically unstable universe in which beliefs and reality itself disintegrate. Both Cicero and Ortega confronted such a situation.

Nineteenth-century liberalism had fostered the notion that man is naturally social and that society is good, when Ortega in fact saw society as a utopian ideal, a seductress who conflicts with man's no less important antisocial impulses. Society, he claimed, is merely the endless attempt of one set of impulses to conquer another. It is not a spontaneous organism as liberalism claims, but a ceaseless pursuit that is essentially degrading because it demands authority and force, both of which must be exercised by those very levels that are better than the task required of them. Ortega now saw liberty as the historically normal form of European life and believed that, even in the face of the curtailment of certain specific freedoms, man could feel himself to be free. For Cicero, however, liberty was indivisible and meant freedom under a strict system of laws. He saw freedom broadly, socially, defined in the answer to the question of who shall rule, whereas modern Europe had seen it in terms of individual limits and man's degree of willingness to allow himself to be ruled. The Roman concept of liberty, then, believed that human nature had to be kept under control, whereas modern liberalism affirmed man's natural goodness and innate sociability. Freedom thus becomes the common agreement to live within a certain system of political inspiration, yet no state, however liberal, can fail to exert pressure.

Ortega postulated three conditions for freedom: a feeling of collective stability; a collective solution that occupies the collective mind and brings about desired change; and universal participation in the functioning of the state. The example of Rome shows to what extent a nation may create its own history, for as the social structure felt new needs, new institutions were developed to deal with them, so that "the State gradually molds itself to the social body as the skin forms itself over our own body" (VI, 100). The pressure and restraint exerted by the state in times of freedom are inseparable from the body itself and are not felt as a lack of liberty, for they best fit the circumstances and the collective preference. Such was the case of the development of Rome as long as the underlying concord existed. Her laws owed more to custom and usage than to abstract reason, and the political institutions that she created responded to a historic need. They were interrelated and sprang from the depths of the collectivity; the liberty that derived from them was part of a total, living system.

Some eight years later, Ortega extended these ideas in *Una interpretación de la historia universal* [An Interpretation of Universal History], twelve lectures primarily intended as an analysis of the first six volumes of Arnold Toynbee's *A Study of History* (1934, 1939). Toynbee claimed that he had been led to his project by the similarity he perceived between trends in contemporary European society and patterns in Graeco-Roman civilization, and aimed to correct many of the errors he found in Spengler's work. Ortega found Toynbee's arguments impressive and significant, but he also found them distressing for Toynbee was in fact treading much of the territory that Ortega had staked out for himself. Ortega sensed another challenge and another opportunity to demonstrate the superiority of his own method of historical reason.[12]

Toynbee's analysis of history had as its basis a theory of historical units which he called "civilizations" that were more inclusive and self-sufficient than nations. For Toynbee, "a civilization is a certain living together of peoples that extends over a determinate space of the planet and that has a beginning and an end in time" (IX, 56). This is the "intelligible historical field" with which the historian could work and in which could be detected the repetition of certain rhythms. Moving backward through time, Toynbee chose the Roman Empire as his example of the universal state. Ortega, however, considered it to be constitutionally abnormal. He claimed that Toynbee was interested only in the surface and, as a result, idealized the imperial structure. Nonetheless, he agreed that its development offered significant similarities to those of contemporary Europe. Such concepts as a world government or a United Nations, he believed, were a demonstration of its enduring effect on men's minds: "The truth, the pure truth is that the Roman Empire has never disappeared from the Western world" (IX, 79).

Ortega preferred to base his own analysis upon two concepts that he believed revealed the very nature of the Roman world: *imperium* and the law. The authority of the Roman emperors, which has served as the basis for all subsequent concentration of legal authority in a single person, was largely the result of human developments, the logic and legality of which were questionable even to those figures most implicated. It was the product of a period that lacked legitimacy, a moment when there was no evident reason for any specific person to hold either the title or the power. Ortega traced this development by applying the narrative method of historical reason to the evolution of the terms *imperium* and *imperator* up to the second century after Christ. What he called the "vexing, dreadful air of constitutive illegitimacy" (IX, 98) that led to the empire could not be caused by any limited faction or people, but had necessarily to be inherent to the entire civilization, and characterized the moment when the collapse of that civilization could be discerned. It was the moment when the law ceased to be seen as just because it was the law and was perceived rather as something that could be altered to suit changing circumstances.

In the most primitive stage in the development of the state, the concept of *imperator* was applied to that person chosen by his society, more or less at random, as the most apt to lead it in its struggle against a specific outside threat. It was intermittent, a reaction to an immediate need, and not rooted in any law. As a society evolves, it necessarily develops a religious concept of its world and in all aspects of Roman life, every act acquired its own religious significance. This led to an attitude that considered only certain people fit for any undertaking because they were favored by the gods. The preeminent figures became religious leaders, whose sphere of competence gradually expanded to include a vast range of social activities. Because such a leader was perceived to have unique attributes, he was seen as indispensable; his role became subject to the law, and he was given a consultative body, the Senate.

The exemplary character of Roman history was partly disrupted by the anomalous expulsion of the Etruscan kings and the institution of the Republic, but Ortega saw the only real alteration in the division of the king's power between two consuls. When the entire Roman populace was needed to defend the nation, they too had to be accorded certain rights in law, thus giving rise to the new state: *Senatus Populusque*, the Senate and the people, jointly. To avoid a recurrence of monarchic abuses, the religious leadership was stripped of political power. This second stage of the Roman legitimacy was more or less democratic in nature, very much like nineteenth-century European ideas of both constitutional monarchy and republic.

The final stage in the evolution of Rome found it in the fullness of its being until about 190 B.C. The Senate had inherited the values and some of the powers of the former monarchy; in it the people perceived the transcendent values of its authority and it became the embodiment of the state, rooted in the past, but pointed toward the future. The new pressures of a growing commercial class, as well as the influx of foreigners and others who had no connection with the traditional ruling families, led to five centuries of growing struggle between patricians and plebeians, the period of discord discussed in *Del Imperio romano* [Concord and Liberty], when a wealth of opportunities had opened to all. A modern period began, and "all modernity is already the beginning of illegitimacy and deconsecration" (IX, 129). The past seemed to recede more quickly. After the victory over Carthage in 204 B.C., Rome fully opened herself to the influences of the outside world, and as Romans ceased to share a common body of beliefs, the consensus that is legitimacy began to evaporate.

In the century after the second Punic war, even the widespread faith in the Roman legal system was severely weakened as the prestige of the Senate was eroded and Rome experienced a series of popular uprisings provoked by a belief that there were sufficient new benefits for everyone. Gradually, a period of civil wars ensued as the disintegration of concord brought about a general air of criminality. Since no one appeared to have an obvious right to lead the state, the personalization of individual Romans had as its natural consequence the personalization of claims to command. Only exhaustion provided a solution: once again Rome felt that anyone could serve as leader, without the need for a judicial basis. The will of the individual was subsumed by the demands of the state as Augustus, against his own wishes, became emperor.

Ortega rejected Toynbee's theory that the origin of Graeco-Roman civilization was to be found in Aegean civilization. Rather, he looked to Mesopotamia, which did not represent Greece's paternity, as Toynbee's system would require, but rather a "universal influence," a widespread current of civilization, the limits of which are all but impossible to define. Ortega saw the essential historical flow less as a direct inheritance of one civilization from another than as a question of these universal influences, civilizations that, while "original," carried within them their primitive and "uncivilized" past. This approach, he claimed, differed in important ways from the arbitrary divisions that Toynbee established between primitivism and civilization. Toynbee, unlike Ortega, did not consider primitive societies to be historically intelligible or dynamic units and thus was unable to deal with the essential historical continuity that was the forte of historical reason. Moreover, Toynbee saw the birth of civilization as a dramatic response to radically altered circumstances by means of the creation of new forms of life. Ortega, however, insisted that man is constitutionally unadapted and inadaptable. His fantasy pushes him on to accept new challenges, and the drama of his existence lies in partial adaption and the resulting creation of new situations to which he must learn to adjust. This led Ortega to conclude that "human life appears to us as it permanently is: a dramatic confrontation and struggle of man with the world, and not a mere occasional maladjustment that occurs at some moments" (IX, 190). Toynbee's doctrine of challenge and response was limited to specific situations to which civilizations reacted, while Ortega saw man as living in a state of eternal aspiration to happiness, always in search of what he does not already possess.

Neither did he accept that geography, as Toynbee would have it, determines the character of a people.[13] It is rather a part of a people's circumstance, offering both obstacles and opportunities. More important than the effect of the land upon man is the reaction that man displays toward the land and what it offers to the aspirations that are his way of being. Ortega insisted that geography does not mold character, but rather that character responds in a particular and revealing way to its environment. Of such reactions is history made: man's response to the opposition that he encounters in his world.

VI *The Individual in Society*

El hombre y la gente [Man and People, 1949–55] represents more than twenty years of thought, having its development in many lectures and courses that Ortega gave over the last two decades of his life.[14] Moved by what he considered to be the inadequacy of both sociology and linguistics, he employed an orientation that was clearly more sociological than historical as he attempted to determine whether society could be taken as an "irreducible reality" or whether the proper object of analysis was the individual.

The "social fact," he again observed, does not preexist in the individual, but is the result of the interrelationship between an individual, who acts through his relationship with his circumstance, and other individuals who do likewise. Ortega distinguished, however, between "interindividual" relationships and truly social ones which reveal themselves in many customs, traditions, and usages that are not the result of either reflection, emotion, or the will of the individual but are imposed on him from without: they are essentially as irrational as they are impersonal. Ortega rejected the idea of a "collective soul" and believed rather that such usages were the product of "the 'inhuman element' in which the person finds himself" (VII, 77). They make social coexistence feasible because they are as predictable in individuals whom one knows as in those whom one does not know. Moreover, they are dictated by the times in which one lives and to which one must therefore rise. Their mechanical nature serves to simplify relationships so that the individual may more easily devote himself to the creative potential of his personal life.

Man's humanness is revealed in his understanding of what he does and why he does it. The things in his world make their presence felt first by means of their corporal resistance to that which is closest to man: his body, in which he is caught and from which he interprets his world. Space is man's primary characteristic; he cannot escape from his "here," and it is this fact that determines his unique perspective. Everything that he encounters occupies, in one way or another, a

certain space that bears a relationship to his own. Likewise, everything has a *being for* (*ser para*) his life, either as an aid or as an
obstacle. Those things that are inextricably involved with man's life
are *prágmata:* their function is related necessarily to the function of
other things and contributes to what Ortega called "pragmatic
fields," of which many may exist in a dynamic relationship in the
world of each person. Each thing encountered is referred to a specific
field, and is for each man either actually, as a presence, or habitually,
as a copresence.

Coexistence is the basis for community, and is possible only when
man and something in his world exist for each other. Upon encounter-
ing another person, man perceives not only the other's corporality,
but through it the signs of an intimacy analogous to his own and that is
in some way expressed in the other's gestures and movements. This
Ortega called the "field of expressivity" (VII, 155). Such intimacy is
not directly revealed, but is rather latent, copresent, and in a constant attempt to emerge from his solitude, man tries to interpret the
other. Ortega continued to find gestures, including speech, to be a
significant and revealing facet of human expression for, whether
conscious or unconscious, they are the key to individual intimacy.[15]
The reality of the other, however, is problematic for man can only
assume that it is in some way like his own. Unlike his own life, it is not
for him a radical reality since it depends on an interpretation, but the
other exists only as a function of the one, as one who reciprocates. His
is still a reality because it is something with which the one must deal,
but it is of a lower order. Nonetheless, individual human life consists
of treating radical realities and many presumed realities as if they
were all equal. Consequently, a great portion of human life is not
authentic because no close examination of its realities normally takes
place. This is perhaps the most startling characteristic of society: "In
solitude man is his truth—in society he tends to be his mere conven-
tionality or falsification" (VII, 144).

Even before he has a consciousness of himself or of the other things
around him, man first perceives the other. From birth, then, man is
altruistic. This is "simple coexistence, the matrix for all possible
'social relationships'" (VII, 150). Gradually, common points of contact
in an "objective world" between the one and the other emerge and
this latter becomes progressively less abstract. The external, "objective" world does not preexist but is the creation of this social relationship. There is still no living together (*convivir*) until there is established a relationship of reciprocal effects so that the one and the other

form a "we" in which the other becomes discernibly unique, a "you." Only then does closeness develop into the intimacy in which we are mutually, to each other (*sernos*).

Each person has a self and a world; this latter is the "not I," but as Ortega pointed out, it is "*my* not I" (VII, 159). The other, however, brings onto our horizon his own self and a "not I" that is uniquely his and that does not communicate with mine. Nonetheless, such other worlds, in their very separateness from mine, form part of my world. Social relationships, then, are predicated upon reciprocity in a common world in which individual worlds coexist. In this "objective" world, man finds that things exist quite independently of him, unlike the things that make up his own world which *are for him*. The objective world is thus enigmatic and provocative, spurring man on to solve its riddles and bringing out in him the sportive sense of life. If other men are the first thing with which an individual finds himself, his first reality is the result of what he sees and hears them say and do: he approaches his own world through his perception of theirs. Man's first authentic reality, then, is social and as such, radically inauthentic, a "pseudoreality" (VII, 178).

Social relationships are determined by the role that others play in my world: whether they help me or hinder me, and society is the tissue of these positive and negative forces. I begin by attributing to the other every possibility, from which I gradually extract the irreplaceable "you," "a definite system of concrete possibilities and concrete impossibilities" (VII, 184). The other becomes copresent: never fully known to me because, like me, he is endlessly in motion, but sufficiently consistent to permit me certain conjectures. However great our intimacy, he will always represent a danger to me insofar as his being is not identical to mine, but, paradoxically, increasing intimacy constantly reminds us of how much the "you" is not "I." It is, then, as a result of social contact, broadly understood, that the authentic nature of the individual "I" emerges. Gradually, the individual becomes more aware of the limits of his "I": he does not begin by perceiving the other as an *alter ego*, but rather sees himself as an *alter tu* (VII, 196).

Beyond this "interindividual" level of relationships extends the truly social, the relationship with the collectivity, where the role of the individual as such has virtually no significance. This is the domain of actions not determined by any person, and therefore, essentially irrational. Ortega posed the critical question: "Is society, then, a peculiar intermediate reality between man and nature, neither one

thing nor the other, but somewhat the one and very much the other?"
(VII, 200).[16]

Usages are elements of historical reason. Some are mechanical,
imposed upon us all, and form part of the world in which we live.
Should we neglect to join in observing them, there is always the
implicit threat of some sort of reprisal. Certain usages are employed
with those others who are less clearly individualized and thus potentially more dangerous, for they serve to indicate a mutual disposition
to abide by normal rules of conduct. It is obvious that most usages
have an "etymology," a meaning that was once real but that has
degenerated into a simple convention. All usages must have origi-
nated in an individual, but they become mechanized in society. They
reflect a reality that is constitutionally slow to change, just as it was
constitutionally slow in being adopted. Social conduct, then, is often
characterized by its lack of contemporary reference, its essentially
anachronistic quality. Most usages are "weak and diffuse" and float
through social life, appearing and fading only at the slowest possible
rate; but a limited number may be "strong and rigid," imposed
forcefully by some concentrated social authority, and can be adopted
and abandoned with considerable haste.

Language was the usage that most attracted Ortega's interest.[17] All
language is a social convention, developed to communicate between
individual solitudes, but the diversity of languages as well as the
diversity within a language are all signs of differing social perceptions.
The significance, the reality of words, comes only from their
expression, a social act that derives from the vital context in which
they are uttered.[18] Ortega distinguished between speaking, which
he considered to be largely irrational, a function of the social context,
a mechanical action that originates outside the individual; and saying,
which precedes and in no way presupposes the existence of language
and is the individual's attempt to exteriorize his intimacy. From the
intimate need springs language which, it is hoped, will make individual expression possible. Nonetheless, Ortega saw that the conven-
tionality of language also twists back to affect and even limit man's
ability to think by removing certain possibilities from his sphere of
thought.

Unlike other animals, man has developed an articulated language
because of this need to communicate the intimacy that he alone
possesses. He is an "abnormal animal" (VII, 253), the richness of
whose imaginative powers demands interpretation. Language is always the tension between the social and the individual, and the

mother tongue is each man's first social instrument; he carries it always within himself, and through it he belongs inescapably to a series of social conventions. Creativity occurs when the individual encounters the limits of the language that society has imposed upon him and must find other ways of expressing his "I," by means not only of words and sounds, but also of gestures.

The use of language, like most other usages, does not normally reflect man's authenticity, for he tends to employ it as he has heard it, without rethinking, except on rare occasions, the subterranean meanings that it contains. Language exemplifies the dominant opinions (*vigencias*) of a society, in contrast with truly personal opinions that can be explained and defended and are genuine "ideas."[19] Dominant usages and opinions are largely self-sustaining: they simply impose themselves on everyone. This, believed Ortega, showed that, on the one hand, society is an inescapable set of forces, but on the other, social usages provide a solid and scarcely changeable reality on which man can depend in order to determine his individual behavior. Society is public power to an extent that goes far beyond institutionalized structures, and some such tensions exist throughout even the most primitive of societies: "The collectivity—without proposing to do so—watches over every minute of individual life" (VII, 268). Such power is a force that counteracts other forces that go against the dominant opinions. Ortega concluded that society is "*constitutively* sick" (ibid.) because it represents the endless struggle between these two types of force, the institutional derivative of which is the state, charged with the task of enforcing public power.[20]

VII   *The Future of the Continent*

Appropriately, Ortega's last major work looked to the future. *Meditación de Europa* [Meditation on Europe] is a revised but unfinished version of ideas presented in a lecture in Berlin in 1949, as well as in other talks and an article in the final years of Ortega's life. In those moments when the Continent was striving to recover from two decades of tension and war, the Free University in West Berlin seemed to be the appropriate locale for an intellectual to attempt to clarify the current European situation. The fundamental values upon which European civilization rests had been weakened, but Ortega was persuaded that the deepening crisis could be healthy: "I do not recall that any civilization has died from an attack of doubt" (IX, 251). Nowhere was such potential for creation more luminous than in defeated and divided Germany, whom he addressed from the viewpoint of a society accustomed to defeat, but always ready to face life on its own terms.

For nine centuries, European reality had been one of coexistence in a common atmosphere defined less by geography than by history. It constituted a society not because of laws or other abstractions, but because it had been "the living together of men within a determined system of usages" (IX, 257), and this reality predated any national units, all of which were the result of denser "socialization" that had arisen from these usages. Ortega believed, however, that the time for nations had passed and that the people of Europe must look not toward "international" units, as Toynbee suggested, but toward an "ultranational" one (IX, 266). History moves inexorably toward larger social units. Whereas, for example, the Graeco-Roman concept of *polis*, city, was characterized by its limited physical size and a con-sequent lack of historical depth, the modern European concept of nation embraced a conviction that a large group that extends beyond what any individual may know directly, possesses a depth, a latency, and a potential that will permit large achievements. A city reveals its potential on the surface, but a nation implies a faith in resources that may yet be concealed. A city is the present, a firmly organized state with a concrete purpose, but a nation is a projection into the future, a gradual accumulation that may become also a state. A city is founded and created, whereas a nation, as the word reveals, is born and exists before and regardless of the will of its members.[21] Whereas Toynbee saw nationhood as a blend of tribalism and democracy, Ortega noted that, in most of Europe, nations had existed for at least two centuries before the rise of democracy, the effect of which had been to deform nationalizing impulses into their opposite, political principles, nationalism. With the rise of modern nationalism, nationality had become a standard. Each nation considered its unique form to be superior, but in so doing it also recognized its coexistence with other nationalities.

Ortega discerned that, since the Middle Ages, European man had lived on two levels: a limited, local level, and a broad, continental level, shared with other peoples. There existed a European way of life, a European state that did not correspond to national divisions, yet underlay all of them. For centuries, the real government of Europe had been that of the "balance of Power" (IX, 295), a plurality that had ruled the continent to a much greater extent than all the individual governments of the various national states, the independence of which Ortega considered to be illusory: "many bees and a single flight" (IX, 296). All nationhoods would have been impossible without the fundamental reality of Europe, the web of usages and prejudices, tradition and culture that are European man.

In the present, Ortega found that this common web was in danger of disintegrating under the weight of the struggle between attempts to impose traditional principles and to impose new ones. The fact that there was felt a need to fight for them revealed that they were not yet or not any longer the truly vigorous usages upon which societies must rest. The resulting lack of authority had thrust Europe into a state of war for several decades, both between and within nations. At the same time as nations found themselves physically closer, a greater spiritual and moral distance had developed. The effect of foreign opinion was becoming unduly great, providing a sort of ill-informed, unarmed intervention that led nations to become closed and defensive. The new current of internationalism, which Toynbee represented, had to be made to recognize that the future of Europe lay in the gradual unification of the continent, not on the basis of the traditional concept of nations, but on a basis of the usages that all her nations shared and that transcended outdated differences.

CHAPTER 7

Conclusion

I T MUST be said that, although it is convenient to divide Ortega's thought into stages, it is no less true that he made of himself an exceptionally organic thinker. The radical changes that took place at various points in his career, while often reflecting the most recent developments in Western thought, were never the results of mere caprice or fashion. Like few other thinkers, Ortega was able to absorb and incorporate change into an overall intellectual structure, the very essence of which was its openness and its legitimate relationship with contemporary concerns. This is not to suggest a facile flexibility, but rather to claim that the practical application of his philosophy was central to that philosophy.

Ortega's style was the ideal medium both to transmit his own insights and to absorb change. Repeatedly and justifiably accused of not completing his studies, Ortega was nevertheless on solid ground in everything that he wrote. Regardless of the reader's reaction to the ideas set forth, these ideas invariably presuppose a scrupulous documentation and a total sincerity on Ortega's part when he affirms them. As a result, his style acquires a warmth and a vibrancy that give life to its brilliancy, imparting a massive quality to his writings that can easily mislead the critic. However, his stylistic self-confidence is intimidating and is accompanied by a tendency to quote himself in order to demonstrate a continuity that is not always present, rather than an evolution. Whereas Unamuno took pride in his contradictions, which were often more apparent than real, and cultivated them as an identifying characteristic of his work, Ortega strove to conceal his contradictions, regardless of how natural and human they might in fact be. This frequently led him into the role of a revisionist reader of his own texts, particularly when he wanted to demonstrate that he was the first to give voice to a certain idea or approach. Only in the publication in 1916 of *Personas, obras y cosas* do we find clear examples of a willingness to admit the inacceptability of youthful ideas that

150

no longer corresponded to his more mature thought. As his reputation grew and his position became more secure, insufficient older ideas were largely ignored, or he strove to find in them meanings and resonances which, while undoubtedly contributing to his newer positions, almost certainly had not meant for him at the time of writing what he claimed for them at a later date. He did not, in fact, apply to himself the principles of historic reason that would have permitted him to write an "Ortega from Within."

Yet let there be no mistake: Ortega y Gasset possessed a greatness of mind that became a historical fact in twentieth-century Spain. He has been accused, often with reason, of superficiality and intellectual vanity, yet the fact remains that he opened the doors of Spain, as he intended, to ways of thinking that might otherwise never have penetrated the Peninsula. Germany had been his major foreign stimulus, as it should have been, for it had been an inescapable element of his circumstance and offered lessons from which Spain could benefit, but his impact would not have been significantly different had he chosen to study in England, France, or America. Ortega was always Spanish and foreign lessons were seen in relation to the Spanish reality. It is this combination that gave him an irreplaceable perspective which, combined with his mental and stylistic agility, could not and cannot be ignored. Like Unamuno, he became part of the Spanish conscience by demonstrating that, whatever one's personal reaction to his work, it was indeed possible to think in Spanish.

He was not a journalist except in the sense that the vast majority of his works were published first in periodicals and that, in fact, he never wrote a complete book. This, however, was a sincere personal response to a historical moment. He repeated frequently that Spain was not able to deal with serious ideas and that it was necessary first to prepare the ground. Had he been born fifty years later, there can be no question but that the entire shape of his production would have been different. At the time, though, journalism reached more Spaniards than books did, and Ortega's philosophy is no less coherent or authentic because it appeared first in newspapers. Rather, the very level of journalism was raised by his presence and example as it was seen that newspapers need not limit themselves to recapitulating the events of the previous day, but that they could be used to foment thought. Ortega's presence attracted other intellectuals to the columns of Spanish newspapers and periodicals and raised the level of those who were already there. He proved that Spain did indeed have in her midst people capable of thinking clearly and writing lucidly about subjects of enduring importance. In 1902, the *Revista de Occidente* would have been an unthinkable venture in Spain, but by 1923, after the experience of *Faro, Europa,* and *España,* it was not. Spain was not on the same plane as her most advanced European neighbors, but the distance had been immeasurably reduced. The Generation of 1898 had prodded the Spanish soul in the first decade of the century, but had been unable to propose concrete solutions. The generation of Ortega built on their concerns and, to a large extent, contributed to a further development of the older generation, with whom it had more in common than has generally been recognized. Ortega and his contemporaries failed to create the perfect nation, but they showed beyond any doubt that it was possible, with discipline, clarity, and good faith, to understand the tensions and aspirations of a country in a period of desperate transition.

The events of the last two decades of Ortega's life would have totally silenced a lesser man and Ortega's withdrawal from public life is hardly surprising. Every event seemed to be proof of the absurdity of his efforts, yet the intellectual imperative was, as he had always claimed, irresistible, and he worked unceasingly. The results have been slow in coming, but undeniable nonetheless. Ortega is a living part of the vital horizon of the Spanish-speaking world, a phenomenon that provides the key to its reality.

His standing among the great philosophers of the West remains to be determined by another age. His ideas are rarely difficult and the clarity of his style, when it does not merely dazzle, serves to facilitate the reader's task. Yet, in his concern to be original, he was often guilty of neglecting to be thorough. Few serious thinkers can have been so consistent in their refusal to see their intuitions and insights through to their logical conclusions. This fact in Ortega made it possible for so many conflicting critical approaches to exist side by side, with equal claims upon our allegiance. It is not enough even to rely on the primary texts, for the fact remains that Ortega did not say enough about almost any important subject. He allowed himself to be intellectually alluring, and all too often moved on, failing to complete even the project at hand, into which he had seduced the reader with unfulfilled promises. Yet his thought is evocative, and that is no small gift. Even in his most pessimistic works, he saw life as aesthetic and intellectual enjoyment; the scope of his enthusiasm was universal, but the ceaseless creation of introductory studies of themes left the door open for succeeding writers to presume conclusions that cannot be easily discarded, although common sense dictates that they are erroneous and ill-intentioned. And yet, he was never dull, never repetitive, never false, and never intellectually careless. He is one of the pillars of a new Spanish intellectual tradition. As Antonio Machado declared, he is "a new gesture."[1]

Notes and References

Chapter One

1. See Giner de los Ríos's opening address for the 1880–81 school year, in *Ensayos*, ed. Juan López-Morillas (Madrid: Alianza, 1969), pp. 102–17.

2. For an indication of the state of philosophical studies in the Spain of the late nineteenth century, see Lutoslawski's report (1897), reproduced in Francisco Romero, *Ortega y Gasset y el problema de la jefatura espiritual* (Buenos Aires, 1960), pp. 124–34.

3. See Manuel Ortega y Gasset, *"El Imparcial." Biografía de un gran diario* (Zaragoza: Librería General, 1956).

4. Eduardo Ortega y Gasset, "Mi hermano José: recuerdos de infancia y mocedad," *Cuadernos Hispanoamericanos* XV:iii (May–June 1956): 189. See also Manuel Ortega y Gasset, *Niñez y mocedad de Ortega* (Madrid, 1964), pp. 35–36.

5. Ortega's semiautobiographical alter ego, Rubín de Cendoya, was also born in Córdoba, and Ortega said of himself, "I am half Andalusian." See *Obras completas* (Madrid, 1966–73), IX, 109; 1948. Unless otherwise indicated, all references to Ortega's work will be to this edition, and will be included in the text. Where appropriate, the date of composition will also be given.

6. Eduardo Ortega y Gasset, p. 199.

7. Ibid., p. 202.

8. See letter to Navarro Ledesma, 9 August 1905, in "Cartas inéditas a Navarro Ledesma," *Cuadernos del Congreso para la Libertad de la Cultura* 66 (November 1962): 18; also "Al margen del libro *A.M.D.G.*," I, 532–35; 1910.

9. Eduardo Ortega y Gasset, p. 195.

10. Manuel Ortega y Gasset, p. 70.

11. Miguel de Unamuno, "Almas de jóvenes," *Obras completas* (Madrid, 1966), I, 1148–59.

12. See Domingo Marrero, *El centauro. Persona y pensamiento de Ortega y Gasset* (1951; 2nd ed. Santurce, Puerto Rico, 1974), p. 192.

13. See letter to Navarro Ledesma, p. 13.

14. "Prólogo para alemanes," VIII, 26; 1934.

15. For the story of his discovery of Dilthey, see "Guillermo Dilthey y la idea de la vida," VI, 165–214; 1933–34.

16. See "Prólogo para alemanes," VIII, 29–30.

17. See Pío Baroja, *Obras completas* (Madrid: Plenitud, 1947), VII, 755; Juan Ramón Jiménez, "Recuerdo a José Ortega y Gasset," *Clavileño* 24 (November–December 1953): 49.

18. Manuel Ortega y Gasset, pp. 12, 89.

19. See Gonzalo Redondo, *Las empresas políticas de José Ortega y Gasset: "El Sol," "Crisol," "Luz" (1917–1934)*, 2 vols. (Madrid, 1970).

20. See Evelyne López-Campillo, *"La Revista de Occidente" y la formación de minorías* (Madrid: Taurus, 1972), pp. 60, 66.

21. See Walter Starkie, *Spanish Raggle-Taggle* (London: John Murray, 1934), pp. 445–46; Max Aub, *La calle de Valverde* (1961; rpt. Barcelona: Seix Barral, 1970), pp. 333–41.

22. See López-Campillo, pp. 74–76.

23. Vicente Romano García notes that in 1926 his name appeared in the *Guide to Society and Nobility in Spain*. See *José Ortega y Gasset, publicista* (Madrid, 1976), p. 229.

24. See *El Sol*, 21 November 1928, p. 2.

25. See *El Sol*, 20 January 1929, p. 1.

26. See *El Sol*, 23 March 1929, p. 1.

27. See Luis Araquistain, "José Ortega y Gasset: Profeta del fracaso de las masas," *Leviatán* 8 (December 1935): 16.

28. Jean Bécarud and Evelyne López-Campillo say that it was published first in *La Tierra* on February 9. See *Los intelectuales españoles durante la II República* (Madrid: Siglo Veintiuno de España, 1978), p. 25.

29. See Manuel Azaña, *Memorias políticas y de guerra* (Barcelona: Editorial Crítica, 1978), I, 323.

30. Ibid., I, 424.

31. See Bécarud and López-Campillo, pp. 81–84; José Antonio Primo de Rivera, "La política y el intelectual. Homenaje y reproche a Ortega," *Obras completas* (Madrid: n.p., 1942), pp. 459–64.

32. Some of the excitement is described by Edith F. Helman, "On Humanizing Education: Ortega's Institute of the Humanities, Madrid, 1948–50," *Hispania* XXIV (1951): 47–50.

33. Heidegger provided a gracious recollection of his meetings with Ortega in "Encuentros con Ortega y Gasset," *Clavileño* VII, no. 39 (1956): 1–2.

34. See Franz Niedermayer, *José Ortega y Gasset*, trans. Peter Tirner (New York, 1973), pp. 81–83.

35. Letter dated January 20, 1955, quoted in Eduardo Ortega y Gasset, p. 203.

36. See Carlos Rojas, *Diez figuras ante la Guerra Civil* (Barcelona, 1973), pp. 373–74.

37. Niedermayer, pp. 100–102.

Chapter Two

1. In a series of articles published in *ABC* in the same month, Azorín also changed his previous denomination from the "Generation of 1896" to the "Generation of 1898." See Azorín, *Obras completas* (Madrid: Aguilar, 1948), II, 896–914.

2. See "¿Hombres o ideas?," I, 439–42. In 1906, Unamuno had written to Ortega: "Every day ideas and things matter less to me, every day feelings and men matter more to me." See "Epistolario entre Unamuno y Ortega," *Revista de Occidente* 19 (1964): 3–4.

3. Ciriaco Morón Arroyo considers this break to have been one of the most important events for the development of Spanish philosophy in this century. See *El sistema de Ortega* (Madrid: 1968), pp. 72, 297. The relationship between the two Titans has been extensively studied, but much remains to be said.

4. See "Los problemas nacionales y la juventud," X, 113.

5. For notes regarding Unamuno's and Ortega's concern for reform in Spain, see Robert McClintock, *Man and His Circumstances: Ortega as Educator* (New York, 1971), pp. 502–509.

6. See "Pidiendo una biblioteca," I, 81–85; 1908; and also the first part of Baroja's *El árbol de la ciencia* (1911).

7. In 1924, even before reading the *Meditations on Quixote,* Curtius would write to Ortega that Germany needed the balance of "Latino-Mediterranean culture," and especially that of Spain (12 March 1924). See "Epistolario entre Ortega y Curtius," *Revista de Occidente* 6 (1963): 330.

8. Toward the end of his life, Ortega would declare: "Socialism . . . does not recognize the values of culture. It does not accept science except insofar as it places itself at the service of the proletarian class, and it adopts an analogous attitude toward letters and the arts," VIII, 669; 1953.

9. Joaquín Costa wrote an article in 1876 called "La política antigua y la política nueva," which was a study of a book by the same title by Giner de los Ríos. See Rafael Pérez de la Dehesa, *El pensamiento de Costa y su influencia en el 98* (Madrid: Sociedad de Estudios y Publicaciones, 1966), p. 69.

10. This striking image, which would become so important, had already appeared in the "Prospectus," I, 304.

11. See "A. Aulard: *Taine, historien de la Révolution Francaise,*" I, 86–90; 1908; "Renan," I, 443–67; 1909; "La teología de Renan," I, 133–36; 1910.

12. The image of Paradise, although not the idea that it represented, disintegrated for Ortega in later years. By 1932, he could elaborate more systematically the concept and declare that, in fact: "The world into which man is thrown when he leaves Paradise is the real world because it is composed of resistances to man, of things that surround him and with which he does not know what to do, because he does not know to what to attend

regarding them. . . . The world . . . is anti-Paradise." See *Unas lecciones de metafísica* (Madrid, 1974), p. 118.

13. See his comments in "La *Sonata de estío* de don Ramón del Valle-Inclán," I, 19–27; 1904. For his recurring ideas regarding the nature of the Mediterranean mind and its culture, see also "El 'pathos' del sur," I, 499–502; 1910, and "Reflexiones de centenario," IV, 25–47; 1924.

14. See Julián Marías, *Ortega. Circunstancia y vocación*, 2 vols. (Madrid, 1973), I, 158, n. 65.

15. For similar reasons, he will apply the same word to Goya in 1948.

16. See Philip W. Silver, "La estética de Ortega," *Nueva Revista de Filología Hispánica* XXII (1973): 294.

17. Ortega returned frequently to the importance of metaphor as an artistic and intellectual tool. See "Renan," I, 454; "Las dos grandes metáforas," II, 387–400; 1924, and, for its importance in his own work, *La idea de principio en Leibniz*, VIII, 292; 1947, and especially note 6. See also Marías, op. cit., II, 41–72.

18. See "Azorín: primores de lo vulgar," II, 158–91.

19. See Julián Marías, "Comentario," to his edition of *Meditaciones del Quijote* (Madrid, 1957), p. 219.

20. See Morón Arroyo, pp. 28, 101–102. The influence of Wilhelm Schapp is explored by Nelson Orringer in "Luminous Perception in *Meditaciones del Quijote*: Ortega's Source," *Revista Canadiense de Estudios Hispánicos* II, no. 1 (1977): 1–26.

21. Von Uexküll's *Umwelt und Innenwelt der Tiere* was published in 1909, and Ortega acknowledged its influence in 1913. Morón Arroyo, p. 148, disagrees that "Adán en el Paraíso" reveals any germ of Ortega's idea of circumstance. See also Marías, *Ortega*, II, 112–19.

22. *Ortega*, II, 128.

23. See Orringer, passim, and especially Philip W. Silver, *Ortega as Phenomenologist: The Genesis of "Meditations on Quixote"* (New York, 1978), pp. 115–49.

24. Morón Arroyo, p. 145.

Chapter Three

1. Ortega's analysis of war's contribution to life was later outlined in "La interpretación bélica de la historia," II, 525–36; 1925.

2. See Evelyne López-Campillo, "Ortega: *El Imparcial* y las Juntas," *Revista de Occidente* 75 (1969): 311–17.

3. For his earlier (1908) ideas on this matter, see "Epistolario de Ortega con Maragall," *Revista de Occidente* 18 (1964): 261–71; and "Renan," I, 461; 1909.

4. Morón Arroyo (p. 440) says that "the biologist stage was a tremendous detour by the thinker."

5. Ortega gave systematic form to his axiology in "Introducción a una estimativa," VI, 315–35; 1923.

6. It is also in part an extension of ideas expressed in "En un banquete en su honor en 'Pombo,'" VI, 226–29; 1922.

7. As Morón Arroyo, p. 116, points out, here Ortega favors rationalism, while in *El tema de nuestro tiempo* he favored vitalism.

8. Ortega was instrumental in having Einstein speak in Madrid in 1923 and published him in the *Revista de Occidente* in 1929.

Chapter Four

1. On at least one occasion, José was confused with his brother, who was having dramatic political problems. The misunderstanding led to an impassioned protest from the *Diario Nacional*, in Bogotá. See "Ortega y Gasset, acusado," in *Repertorio Americano* X, no. 7 (20 April 1925): 101.

2. In December 1925 and January 1926 he published a series entitled "Maura o la política," which represented his return to political commentary and served for the lessons in "Mirabeau." In August 1926 he also looked briefly at Julius Caesar, whom he considered another political genius. See II, 546–47.

3. See, for example, "El origen deportivo del estado," II, 607–23; 1924.

4. This was, of course, the moment of great popular interest stimulated by the discovery of and controversy surrounding the opening in Egypt of the tomb of King Tutankhamun.

5. Ortega was clarifying his concept of historiography in "Hegel y América," II, 563–76; 1928, and "La *Filosofía de la Historia* de Hegel y la historiología," IV, 521–41; 1928.

6. See Leon Livingstone, "Ortega y Gasset's Philosophy of Art," *PMLA* LXVII (1952): especially pp. 629–34.

7. The beginnings of these ideas can be found in "Musicalia," II, 325–44; 1921, and "Apatía artística," II, 334–39; 1921.

8. He attacked the new art in "¿Qué pasa en el mundo?," *Luz*, 1 and 3 June 1933.

9. In 1927, E. M. Forster wa also to insist on characters' ability to surprise in the novel. See *Aspects of the Novel* (London: Pelican Books, 1966), p. 85.

10. The *Obras completas* give the almost certainly incorrect date of May 1924. For Ortega's earliest reaction to Freud, see "Psicoanálisis, ciencia problemática," I, 216–36; 1911.

11. As Morón Arroyo points out (p. 182), the term derives from Max Scheler.

12. See also "Para la cultura del amor," II, 140–44; 1917; "Para una psicología del hombre interesante," IV, 467–80; 1925, and "Para la historia del amor," III, 439–45; 1926. Ortega wrote frequently about the essence of femininity. See, for example, "Divagación ante el retrato de la Marquesa de

Santillana" (1918), "Esquema de Salomé" (1921), "Epílogo al libro *De Francesca a Beatrice*" (1924), "Paisaje con una corza al fondo" (1927), "La percepción del prójimo" (1929) and *El hombre y la gente* (1949–50). The theme was in the air: in 1926, Gregorio Marañón published *Tres ensayos sobre la vida sexual,* which received considerable attention.

13. He used as his basis fragments that would reappear in "Defensa del teólogo frente al místico," which was itself a section of *¿Qué es filosofía?*

14. Later, he wrote: "The fact is that the most effective, permanent, genuine and radical intervention of woman in history takes place in this dimension of love," *En torno a Galileo,* V, 49; 1933.

15. See Morón Arroyo, p. 45 and passim; José Gaos, *Sobre Ortega y Gasset* (Mexico, 1957), pp. 16, 78–81. In 1929, Ortega wrote to Curtius: "I am now entering—for the first time—into formal production. I would like to give a lot in a short time . . . ," "Epistolario entre Ortega y Curtius," *Revista de Occidente* 6 (1963): 355.

16. This is developed in "El origen deportivo del estado," II, 607, and again in "Vicisitudes en las ciencias," IV, 63–68; 1930, and "Bronca en la física," V, 271–87; 1937.

17. Ortega himself also referred to two lectures to the Association of Friends of Art in Buenos Aires in 1928, and at least three articles published in *El Sol* in 1925 and 1926: "La resurrección de la mónada," "Sobre el fascismo," "Dinámica del tiempo: masas." Ortega incorrectly attributes the last to 1926; the exact date of publication was May 8, 1927. To these articles must be added "Democracia morbosa" (1917), "Muerte y resurrección" (1917), "No ser hombre ejemplar" (1924), "La política por excelencia" (1927), "Tierras del porvenir" (1927), "El poder social" (1927). See also Manuel Durán, "Tres definidores del hombre-masa: Heidegger, Ortega, Riesman," *Cuadernos Americanos* XV: ii (1956): especially pp. 77–78, for other influences and parallels.

18. Toward the end of his life, the growth of state organizations would continue to concern him. See "Individuo y organización," IX, 677–90; 1953.

19. One of the most interesting reviews in English of Ortega's book is H. L. Mencken's "Spanish Katzenjammer," *Nation,* 21 September 1932, p. 260.

20. By 1954, Ortega would be able to declare that "the University has stopped being a prominent factor in our society and vegetates on very secondary levels in collective life," IX, 730.

Chapter Five

1. See José Montero Alonso, "'El error Berenguer,' de José Ortega y Gasset," *Gaceta de la Prensa* no. 156 (15 June 1964): 32–42.

2. See Ramón Pérez de Ayala, "Al Servicio de la República," in *Escritos políticos* (Madrid: Alianza, 1967), pp. 215–36.

3. "A Spaniard on Spain," *The Living Age,* October, 1931, p. 148.

4. Ibid., p. 145.

5. Ibid., p. 148.

6. Ibid., p. 147. Azaña made his controversial declaration in Parliament on October 13, 1931.

7. The Constituent Parliament, for example, first met on Bastille Day, 1931.

8. See Manuel Azaña, I, 323.

9. Introduction to his translation of *The Mission of the University* (Princeton: Princeton University Press, 1944), p. 6. See also the article cited by José Antonio Primo de Rivera.

10. All references are to *Unas lecciones de metafísica* (Madrid, 1974).

11. Ortega examined the concrete nature of personal vocation as applied to one's life work in "Sobre las carreras," V, 167–83; 1934.

12. Egon Schwarz, for example, has commented: "What Ortega is after is not so much a new understanding of Goethe, but rather and above all a comprehension of the spirit of his own epoch mirrored in a figure great enough to encompass humanity." See "Ortega y Gasset and German Culture," *Monatshefte* XLIX, no. 1 (January 1957): 91.

13. This was already evident in "¿Por qué se vuelve a la filosofía?" (1913).

14. See "Juan Vives y su mundo," VIII, 507–43; 1940.

15. To some extent, he continued this discussion in "Ensimismamiento y alteración," V, 295–315; 1939, and especially near the end of his life in "El mito del hombre allende la técnica," VIII, 617–24; 1951. See also Arturo García Astrada, *El pensamiento de Ortega y Gasset* (Buenos Aires, 1961), chapter XII.

16. See "Guillermo Dilthey y la idea de la vida," VI, 165–214; 1933–34.

Chapter Six

1. See José Gaos, p. 84; Carlos Rojas, p. 365; Gonzalo Fernández de la Mora, *Ortega y el 98* (Madrid, 1963), p. 167.

2. See "El intelectual y el otro," V, 508–16; 1940.

3. See "Tabla de generaciones," VIII, 660–61; 1947.

4. See Paulino Garagorri's discussion: "En torno al 'Goya' de Ortega," in *Relecciones y disputaciones orteguianas* (Madrid, 1966), pp. 45–60.

5. See also "Prólogo a *Veinte años de caza mayor*," VI, 419–91; 1942, and Julián Marías, "Vida y razón en la filosofía de Ortega" (1945), in *Acerca de Ortega* (Madrid, 1971), pp. 63–97.

6. See, for example, "Meditación del marco," II, 307–13; 1921.

7. Compare Don Quixote and Maese Pedro in *Meditaciones del Quijote*, I, 380–81; also *Ideas sobre la novela* and the need for a closed horizon.

8. For details regarding the writing of this book, see Julián Marías, "Exhortación al estudio de un libro," in *Acerca de Ortega*, pp. 169–74. Morón Arroyo considers it, like *En torno a Galileo*, as another example of Ortega's "introductionism" p. 33), but Garagorri disagrees. See his analysis, "El 'radicalismo' en el pensamiento de Ortega y Gasset," in *Relecciones y*

disputaciones orteguianas, especially p. 32. An insightful discussion of some aspects is offered by García Astrada, chapter IX.

9. Ortega says "intución sensual." I have adopted the term used by Mildred Adams in her translation (New York: W. W. Norton, 1971).

10. Some idea of Ortega's approach to Leibniz can be deduced from the appendix, "Del optimismo en Leibniz." See also "La metafísica y Leibniz," III, 431–34; 1926.

11. Some of his attitudes had appeared in "Sobre la muerte de Roma," II, 537–47; 1926, and he would return to them in "Un capítulo sobre la cuestión de cómo muere una creencia," IX, 707–25; 1954.

12. Other similarities between the thought of Ortega and theories of Toynbee were pointed out, before the publication of Ortega's course, by Gustavo Lagos Matus in *El pensamiento social de Ortega y Gasset* (Santiago de Cuba, 1956), pp. 8–10. Toynbee's response to Ortega's criticisms, despite its *tu quoque* approach, also serves to show how close to the mark the Spaniard was. See Arnold Toynbee, "Sobre una interpretación de Ortega," *Revista de Occidente* 15 (1964): 356–57. See also José Hierro S.-Pescador, *El derecho en Ortega* (Madrid, 1965), chapter V.

13. In particular, he had dealt with man's relationship to his geography in his splendid travel writings. See "De Madrid a Asturias o los dos paisajes," II, 247–63; 1915, and "Temas de viaje," II, 367–83; 1922.

14. He himself referred to a lecture of the same title given in Valladolid in 1934 (IX, 355, n. 1), and the first chapter was published in 1939 as "Ensimismamiento y alteración." See also "El silencio, gran Brahmán," II, 625–33; especially p. 627; "La percepción del prójimo," VI, 153–63; 1929.

15. See "Sobre la expresión, fenómeno cósmico," II, 577–94; 1925; "Vitalidad, alma, espíritu," II, 451–80; 1924.

16. Cf. "The 'I' does not acquire its genuine profile without a 'you' that limits it and a 'we' that serves as a backdrop," I, 529; 1910.

17. See "Fraseología y sinceridad," II, 481–89; 1926; "Miseria y esplendor de la traducción," V, 433–59; 1937; "Comentario al 'Banquete' de Platón," IX, 751–84; 1946. See also Nelson R. Orringer, "Ortega y Gasset's Sportive Theories of Communication," *Modern Language Notes* 85 (1970): 207–34. A reform of linguistics was to be one of the aims of the Institute of Humanities. See VII, 17–18; 1948.

18. Because he felt that the same was true of ideas, he was moved to write his "Prólogo para alemanes" in 1934.

19. See Howard Raley, *José Ortega y Gasset, Philosopher of European Unity* (University, Alabama, 1971), pp. 50–53.

20. See Arturo García Astrada, chapter V. For the relationship with Weber, Durkheim, and Bergson, see León Dujovne, *La concepción de la historia en la obra de Ortega y Gasset* (Buenos Aires, 1968), p. 84.

21. Ortega had discussed the origins of the city in "Pepe Tudela vuelve a la meseta," II, 328–33; 1921.

Chapter Seven

1. Manuel y Antonio Machado, *Obras completas* (Madrid: Editorial Plenitud, 1962), p. 1204.

Selected Bibliography

PRIMARY SOURCES

1. General

"Discursos inéditos" (1932). *Revista de Occidente* 140 (November 1974): 148–65.

Meditaciones del Quijote. Ed. Julián Marías. Madrid: Ediciones de la Universidad de Puerto Rico y Revista de Occidente, 1957.

Obras completas. 11 vols. Madrid: Revista de Occidente, 1966–73.

Sobre la razón histórica. Madrid: Alianza, 1979.

"A Spaniard On Spain." *Living Age,* October 1931, pp. 145–48.

Unas lecciones de metafísica. Madrid: Revista de Occidente, 1974.

2. Correspondence

"Cartas inéditas a Navarro Ledesma." *Cuadernos del Congreso para la Libertad de la Cultura* 66 (1962): 2–18.

"Epistolario de Ortega con Maragall." *Revista de Occidente* 18 (1964): 261–71.

"Epistolario entre Ortega y Curtius." *Revista de Occidente* 6 (1963): 329–41; 7 (1963): 1–27.

"Epistolario entre Unamuno y Ortega." *Revista de Occidente* 19 (1964): 3–28.

Many articles by Ortega have still not been collected. Most may be found listed in Vicente Romano García. *José Ortega y Gasset, publicista.* Madrid: Akal, 1976, pp. 311–33.

SECONDARY SOURCES

ABELLÁN, JOSÉ LUIS. "Aportaciones de Unamuno y Ortega para una filosofía española." *Cuadernos de la Cátedra Miguel de Unamuno* 14–15 (1964–65): 11–18. The shape, purpose, and motivation of the thought of the two philosophers.

———. "El tema de España en Ortega y Unamuno." *Asomante* XVII:4 (1961): 26–40. Unamuno's sense of the religious and intrahistorical leads to a superior sense of the authentic nature of Spain.

———. *Ortega y Gasset en la filosofía española.* Madrid: Tecnos, 1966. A stimulating and personal appreciation of Ortega's position within his time and his contribution to it.

AGUILERA CERNI, VICENTE. *Ortega y d'Ors en la cultura artística española.* Madrid: Raycar, 1966. Ill-focused but often provocative attempt to give structure to Ortega's aesthetics.

ALLUNTIS, FÉLIX. "The 'Vital and Historical Reason' of José Ortega y Gasset." *Franciscan Studies* XV (1955): 60–78. A lucid summary of the major items of Ortega's mature philosophy, plus a scrupulous criticism of its limitations.

ARANGUREN, J. L. *La ética de Ortega*. Madrid: Taurus, 1958. An important analysis by a leading liberal Catholic intellectual.

ARAQUISTAIN, LUIS. "José Ortega y Gasset: Profeta del fracaso de las masas." *Leviatán* 8 (December 1934): 13–22; 9 (January 1935): 1–14. Dramatic rejection of the "anachronistic" historical views of Ortega, as seen from the revolutionary Left.

ARAYA, GUILLERMO. *Claves filológicas para la comprensión de Ortega*. Madrid: Gredos, 1971. Frequently enlightening examination of Ortega's use of genres and speech structures as a basis for a new understanding of his great themes.

AYALA, FRANCISCO. "Ortega y Gasset, crítico literario." *Revista de Occidente* 140 (1974): 214–35. Ortega's concept of literature as related to his philosophy of culture and art.

BASAVE, AGUSTÍN. *Miguel de Unamuno y José Ortega y Gasset. Un bosquejo valorativo*. Mexico: Jus, 1950. Radically different in their personalities, the two approach each other in their existentialism; highly impressionistic approach.

BAYÓN, JULIO. *Razón vital y dialéctica en Ortega*. Madrid: Revista de Occidente, 1972. Ortega as a dialectical materialist in his approach to human life.

BELMONTE, MARINO Y. "Notas sobre los 'principios de las ciencias,' según Ortega y Gasset." *Cuadernos Hispanoamericanos* 137 (1961): 126–39. The philosophical response required by the crisis in the physical sciences; provoked by *La idea de principio en Leibniz*.

BOREL, JEAN-PAUL. *Introducción a Ortega y Gasset*. Trans. Laureano Pérez Latorre. Madrid: Guadarrama, 1969. Carefully considered introduction to both the philosophy as such and the entirety of Ortega's intellectual and social activity.

CASCALÈS, CHARLES. *L'Humanisme d'Ortega y Gasset*. Paris: Presses Universitaires de France, 1957. Competent overview of Ortega's philosophy, as seen through his concept of human life in the individual and in society.

CEPLECHA, CHRISTIAN. *The Historical Thought of José Ortega y Gasset*. Washington: Catholic University of America Press, 1958. Sympathetic Christian view of Ortega as a "secular humanist"; useful biography, with some slight inaccuracies.

CLAVERÍA, CARLOS. "Ortega y su primera interpretación de la historia," in *Spanish Thought and Letters in the Twentieth Century*. Eds. Germán Bleiberg and E. Inman Fox. Nashville: Vanderbilt University Press, 1966, pp. 143–52. An important discussion of Ortega's doctoral thesis.

CONWAY, JAMES I. "Ortega y Gasset's 'Vital Reason.'" *Thought* XXII (1957): 594–602. A criticism of Ortega's thought as seen through that of Marías.

DíAZ, JANET W. *The Major Themes of Existentialism in the Work of José Ortega y Gasset*. Chapel Hill: University of North Carolina Press, 1970. Especially useful for its orientation within the existing bibliography.

DONOSO, ANTÓN. "The Influence of José Ortega y Gasset in Latin America." *Filosofia* (São Paolo) III (1974): 43–49. A useful contribution to an understudied theme.

DUJOVNE, LEÓN. *La concepción de la historia en la obra de Ortega y Gasset*. Buenos Aires: Santiago Rueda, 1968. Narrative recapitulation of the sweep of Ortega's historical concerns.

DURÁN, MANUEL. "Dos filósofos de la simpatía y del amor: Ortega y Max Scheler." *La Torre* 15–16 (1956): 103–18. Love in Ortega as the creation of values; points of contact with Scheler.

―――. "Tres definidores del hombre-masa: Heidegger, Ortega, Riesman." *Cuadernos Americanos* XV:ii (1956): 69–86. Suggestive examination of the crisis of contemporary man from three characteristic viewpoints; intriguing comparisons.

FERNÁNDEZ DE LA CERA, MANUEL. "El epistolario Unamuno-Ortega." *Cuadernos de la Cátedra Miguel de Unamuno* XXII (1972): 103–18. Intermittently perceptive study of the relationship.

FERNÁNDEZ DE LA MORA, GONZALO. *Ortega y el 98*. Madrid: Rialp, 1963. Scrupulously balanced criticism of Ortega's thought as a result of the "spirit of 98" by an admirer whose idol had feet of clay.

FERRATER MORA, JOSÉ. *José Ortega y Gasset: An Outline of His Philosophy*. New Haven: Yale University Press, 2nd. rev. ed., 1963. An elegant, disciplined, peerless overview of the philosophy; indispensable.

GAETE, ARTURO. *El sistema maduro de Ortega*. Buenos Aires: Compañía General Fabril, 1962. The "great questions" of Ortega's post-1928 works, seen from a Christian viewpoint, with some interesting conclusions. Companion volume to that of Larraín Acuña.

GAOS, JOSÉ. *Sobre Ortega y Gasset y otros trabajos de historia de las ideas en España y la América española*. Mexico: Imprenta Universitaria, 1957. Contains five important studies by a disciple who admired Ortega's philosophy but regretted his political decisions, which he nevertheless finds consistent.

GARAGORRI, PAULINO. *Introducción a Ortega*. Madrid: Alianza, 1970. An excellent course (previously published as *Ortega, una reforma de la filosofía*. Madrid: Revista de Occidente, 1958) and two lectures on the essence of Ortega's philosophy, by one of his more scrupulous followers.

―――. *Relecciones y disputaciones orteguianas*. Madrid: Taurus, 1966. Nine articles (1950–65) of varying quality.

―――. *Unamuno, Ortega, Zubiri en la filosofía española*. Madrid: Plenitud, 1968. A convincing attempt at reestablishing Spain as a philosophical land through her three most distinguished practitioners.

GARCÍA ASTRADA, ARTURO. *El pensamiento de Ortega y Gasset*. Buenos Aires: Troquel, 1961. A carefully constructed and skillfully executed analytical summary of Ortega's major philosophical themes. Contains a lexicon of Ortega's terminology.

————. "Ideas políticas de Ortega y Gasset." *Cuadernos Hispanoamericanos* 114 (June 1959): 238–49. Excellent analysis of Ortega's political philosophy.

GUY, ALAIN. *Ortega y Gasset: Critique d'Aristote.* Toulouse: Presses Universitaires de France, 1963. The most thorough discussion to date of *La idea de principio en Leibniz.*

HIERRO S.-PESCADOR, JOSÉ. *El derecho en Ortega.* Madrid: Revista de Occidente, 1965. Articulate investigation of Ortega's attitude toward law in its social, personal, and ideal aspects, with a conclusion based primarily on *Una interpretación de la historia universal.*

HOLMES, OLIVER W. *Human Reality and the Social World: Ortega's Philosophy of History.* Amherst: University of Massachusetts Press, 1975. Ortega's historical thought within its European philosophical context; occasionally inaccurate biography.

IRIARTE, JOAQUÍN. *José Ortega y Gasset. Su personalidad y su doctrina.* Madrid: Razón y Fe, 1942. An early conservative Catholic view, rich in biographical detail and often fair.

LAFUENTE FERRARI, ENRIQUE. *Ortega y las artes visuales.* Madrid: Revista de Occidente, 1970. Intriguing assortment of essays by an outstanding art historian and follower of Ortega.

LAÍN ENTRALGO, PEDRO. "Los católicos y Ortega," in *Ejercicios de comprensión.* Madrid: Taurus, 1959, pp. 57–76. An attempt to restore honor to the dispute over Ortega's attitude toward religion and the Church.

————. "Ortega y el futuro," in *La espera y la esperanza.* Madrid: Revista de Occidente, 1957, 3rd ed. 1962, pp. 437–55. Ortega's views on the future and its significance for life.

LALCONA, JAVIER F. *El idealismo político de Ortega y Gasset.* Madrid: Cuadernos para el Diálogo, 1974. The most thorough study to date of the entire political evolution.

LARRAÍN ACUÑA, HERNÁN. *La génesis del pensamiento de Ortega.* Buenos Aires: Compañía General Fabril, 1962. Readable account of the major developments of Ortega's philosophy up to 1927 and his encounter with the thought of Heidegger.

LIVINGSTONE, LEON. "Ortega y Gasset's Philosophy of Art." *PMLA* LXVII (1952): 609–54. A broad and outstanding development of its theme.

LÓPEZ QUINTÁS, ALFONSO. *El pensamiento filosófico de Ortega y d'Ors, una clave de interpretación.* Madrid: Guadarrama, 1972. An application to Ortega's philosophy of a strict methodology made possible by the very atmosphere that he fostered.

McCLINTOCK, ROBERT. *Man and His Circumstances: Ortega as Educator.* New York: Teachers College Press, 1971. Massive account of Ortega's work and actions seen as social pedagogy.

MARÍAS, JULIÁN. *Acerca de Ortega.* Madrid: Revista de Occidente, 1971.

Uneven but indispensable collection of Marías' most important essays on the Master; a somewhat monolithic vision.

———. "La retracción a España del europeo Ortega." *Revista de Occidente* 140 (1974): 181–95. Ortega's European vision of his inescapable Spanish circumstance.

———. *Ortega. I. Circunstancia y vocación*. Madrid: Revista de Occidente, 1960; 2nd ed., 1972. 2 vols. (English translation by Frances López Morillas. *José Ortega y Gasset, Circumstance and Vocation*. Norman: University of Oklahoma Press, 1970). The most important single work on Ortega by his most faithful disciple. Highly partisan and irreplaceable discussion of his formation and writings before *Meditations on Quixote*. Many other outstanding interpretations of Ortega and his place in the history of Spanish thought can be found throughout Marías's *Obras*. Madrid: Revista de Occidente, 1959–.

MARICHAL, JUAN. "La 'generación de los intelectuales' y la política (1909–1914)." *Revista de Occidente* 140 (1974): 166–80. Ortega as political leader of the emerging Generation of 1914.

———. "La singularidad estética de Ortega," in *La voluntad de estilo*. Madrid: Revista de Occidente, 1971, pp. 207–18. Excellent insight into some peculiarities of Ortega's use of the language.

MARRERO, DOMINGO. *El centauro: persona y pensamiento de Ortega y Gasset*. 1st ed. 1951. Santurce: Universidad de Puerto Rico, 1974. A collection of short pieces, particularly important for information regarding Ortega's studies in Germany.

MORÓN, GUILLERMO. *Historia política de Ortega y Gasset*. Mexico: Oasis, 1956. Forthright early study of Ortega's politics.

MORÓN ARROYO, CIRIACO. *El sistema de Ortega y Gasset*. Madrid: Alcalá, 1968. Luminous insight into the evolution of the totality of Ortega's thought; an indispensable work, of great value for tracing possible philosophical influences.

NIEDERMAYER, FRANZ. *José Ortega y Gasset*. Trans. Peter Tirner. New York: Unger, 1973. Original, but occasionally wrong-headed view of Ortega as thinker and social activist.

ORRINGER, NELSON. "Life as Shipwreck or as Sport in Ortega y Gasset?" *Romance Notes* 17 (1976): 70–75. Good attempt at resolving two apparently contradictory images.

———. "Ortega y Gasset's Sportive Theories of Communication." *Modern Language Notes* 85 (1970): 207–34. Excellent analysis of Ortega's view of language, its demands and limitations.

———. "Ortega y Gasset's Sportive Vision of Plato." *Modern Language Notes* 88 (1973): 264–80. Goes well beyond its title in providing the most nearly complete examination of Ortega's affinity with and reservations about both Plato and his thought.

———. *Ortega y sus fuentes germánicas*. Madrid: Gredos, 1979. An excellent and controversial study of the possible sources of many of Ortega's central concerns, based on his personal library.

ORTEGA Y GASSET, EDUARDO. "Mi hermano José: recuerdos de infancia y mocedad." *Cuadernos Hispanoamericanos* XV:iii (1956): 174–211. Fascinating biographical account by the elder brother.

ORTEGA Y GASSET, MANUEL. *Niñez y mocedad de Ortega.* Madrid: CLAVE, 1964. Equally useful biography by the younger brother.

PELLICANI, LUCIANO. *Introduzione a Ortega y Gasset.* Naples: Ligouri Editore, 1978. A sociopolitical study that sees Ortega as prophet of a renewed type of liberal Socialist democracy.

RALEY, HOWARD C. *José Ortega y Gasset: Philosopher of European Unity.* University: University of Alabama Press, 1971. Ortega's concept of Europe as an integral part and culmination of his entire philosophical development.

RAMÍREZ, SANTIAGO. *La filosofía de Ortega y Gasset.* Barcelona: Herder, 1958. The book, bitterly hostile, that did most to provoke the disputes over the compatibility of Ortega's thought with that of Christianity.

READ, HERBERT. "High Noon and Darkest Night: Some Observations on Ortega y Gasset's Philosophy of Art." *Journal of Aesthetics and Art Criticism* XXIII (1964): 43–50. Stimulating and unconventional reaction by an outstanding art critic.

REDONDO, GONZALO. *Las empresas políticas de José Ortega y Gasset: "El Sol," "Crisol," "Luz" (1917–1934).* 2 vols. Madrid: Rialp, 1970. Luxuriantly detailed account of Ortega's journalistic undertakings and their relationship to his circumstance.

RODRÍGUEZ HUÉSCAR, ANTONIO. *Perspectiva y verdad: el problema de la verdad en Ortega.* Madrid: Revista de Occidente, 1966. Toward a closely argued unification of Ortega's thought through eight stages of his perspectivist view of truth and authenticity.

RODRÍGUEZ-LUIS, JULIO. "La discusión sobre la novela entre Ortega y Baroja." *La Torre* X:38 (1962): 85–125. Competent summary of the points made by each writer.

ROJAS, CARLOS. *Diez figuras ante la Guerra Civil.* Barcelona: Nauta, 1973. Very detailed biographical account of Ortega during and after the Civil War; much new information.

ROMANO GARCÍA, VICENTE. *José Ortega y Gasset, publicista.* Madrid: Akal, 1976. Careful discussion of Ortega's journalism with the most nearly complete listing of his publications; only occasional lapses and inaccuracies.

ROMERO, FRANCISCO. *Ortega y Gasset y el problema de la jefatura espiritual.* Buenos Aires: Losada, 1960. Contains two moving and disciplined articles detailing the nature and results of Ortega's role as a "politician of culture."

RUKSER, UDO. *Bibliografía de Ortega.* Madrid: Revista de Occidente, 1971. The most complete bibliography of works about Ortega, awkwardly arranged by country of publication; needs updating.

SALCEDO, EMILIO. "Unamuno y Ortega. Diálogo entre dos españoles." *Cuadernos de la Cátedra Miguel de Unamuno* VII (1956): 97–130. Fine narrative reconstruction of the contacts between the two men.

SALMERÓN, FERNANDO. *Las mocedades de Ortega y Gasset.* Mexico: El Colegio de México, 1959. The pioneering study on Ortega's work before the *Meditations on Quixote.*

SÁNCHEZ VILLASEÑOR, JOSÉ. *Ortega y Gasset, Existentialist.* Trans. Joseph Small. Chicago: H. Regnery, 1949. Occasionally wrong-headed, but often perceptive Jesuit criticism of Ortega's philosophy as irredeemably relativistic and atheistic.

SCHWARTZ, KESSEL. "Ortega y Gasset and Goethe." *Hispania* XLIII (1960): 320–27. The vital significance of Ortega's view of Goethe.

SHARKEY, JAMES. "Ortega, Einstein and Perspectivism." *Romance Notes* 12 (1970): 21–25. Perspectivism rooted in biological methodology and relativity as an exclusively logical methodology, with preference for the latter.

SILVER, PHILIP W. "La estética de Ortega." *Nueva Revista de Filología Hispánica* 22 (1973): 291–309. Excellent examination of "Ensayo de estética" in the light of Husserlian phenomenology.

———. *Ortega as Phenomenologist: The Genesis of "Meditations on Quixote."* New York: Columbia University Press, 1978. A persuasive account of Ortega's enduring debt to Phenomenology.

SOBEJANO, GONZALO. *Nietzsche en España.* Madrid: Gredos, 1967. Contains an excellent account of Ortega's debt to Nietzsche.

TORRE, GUILLERMO DE. "Ortega, teórico de la literatura." *Papeles de Son Armadans* XIX (1957): 22–46. Stresses the essentially literary impulse behind much of Ortega's writing.

VELA, FERNANDO. *Ortega y los existencialismos.* Madrid: Revista de Occidente, 1961. Of these four articles by the *Revista*'s original secretary, the one lending its title to the collection is of greatest interest.

WALGRAVE, JAN HENRICUS. *La filosofía de Ortega y Gasset.* Trans. Luis G. Daal. Madrid: Revista de Occidente, 1965. Sweeping, admiring, and often rewarding examination of the entire reach of Ortega's career.

Index

ABC, 33
Academia Real de Ciencias Morales y Políticas, 24
Adam, 48, 59
Agrupación al Servicio de la República, 30, 31, 32, 112–16
Alcántara, Francisco, 19
Alfonso XII, 15
Alfonso XIII, 66, 70, 87, 113
Alicante, 33
Altamira, 48
Alvarez, Melquíades, 23
Amsterdam, 33
Aragón, 73, 132
Argentina, 25, 33
Aristocracy, 39, 41, 64, 71, 74–76, 96, 107, 109, 115
Aristotle, 135, 136, 137
Art, 47–49, 54, 55, 58, 76–77, 95–97, 99, 129–33
Asamblea para el Progreso de las Ciencias, 22
Asociación Española para el Progreso de las Ciencias, 34
Aspen, 35
Asturias, 35
Ateneo de Madrid, 34, 133
Augustus Caesar, 142
Azaña, Manuel, 31, 115, 156n29, 161n6, 161n8
Azcárate, Gumersindo de, 23
Azorín, see Martínez Ruiz, José

Bacchus, 134
Balzac, Honoré de, 19
Baroja, Pío, 51–53, 55, 97, 98, 156n17, 157n6; *El árbol de la ciencia*, 51, 157n6

Basque country, 114
Bavarian Academy of Fine Arts, 35
Bayliss, Sir William Maddock, 79
Berenguer, Dámaso, 30, 112
Berlin, 21, 32, 35, 147
Berlin, Free University of, 35, 147
Beyle, Marie Henri, 101–102; *De l'Amour*, 101
"Biblioteca de Ideas del siglo XX," 26, 62
Bilbao, 43
Biologism, 79, 80, 92, 94, 116
Blasco Ibáñez, Vicente, 87
Bologna, 23
Bolshevism, 88, 108, 113
Britain, 35, 86
Buenos Aires, 29, 34, 138
Buenos Aires, University of, 25, 29, 127

Calderón de la Barca, Pedro, 129
Calpe, 26
Canalejas, José, 23
Cano, Alonso, 129
Cánovas de Castillo, Antonio, 15
Capitalism, 41
Carl Augustus, 119
Carthage, 141
Castile, 73
Catalonia, 32, 69, 71, 114
Cato, 30, 112
Cejador y Frauca, Julio, 20
Cervantes Saavedra, Miguel de, 49, 55–61; *Don Quijote de la Mancha*, 18, 55, 58–61
Cézanne, Paul, 96
Chateaubriand, François René, vicomte de, 46

Chile, 29, 33
Christianity, 83, 121
Cicero, 138–39; *De re publica*, 138
Circumstance, 55–61, 83, 106, 117, 122, 142–43
Civilization, 51, 67, 79, 80, 107, 142
Civil War, 26–28, 32, 34
Classicism, 47
Cohen, Hermann, 21, 23, 99
Cologne, 20
Colomer, Gonzalo, 19
Colomer, Luis, 19
Comisión Parlamentaria del Estado, 31
Congreso de Ciencias, 23
Conservatism, 39
Conservative Party, 45, 66
Constitution of 1876, 66, 70, 90–91
Constitution of 1931, 31
Córdoba, 18, 19, 155n5
Córdoba (Argentina), 25
Costa, Joaquín, 16, 17, 37, 157n9
Crisol, 30, 31
Cuba, 35
Cubism, 96
Culture, 42–44, 45, 46–47, 57, 58–59, 79, 80, 81–82, 85, 94, 109–11, 118, 122
Curtius, Ernst Robert, 32, 157n7

Dante, 96
Darmstadt, 35
Decadentism, 50
Delft, 33
Democracy, 65, 67, 68, 71, 86, 89, 106–107, 148
Descartes, René, 33, 81, 84, 96, 105, 121, 129, 132, 135–38
Deusto, University of, 19, 20, 29
Dictatorship, 27, 28–30, 86–88, 90, 112
Dilthey, Wilhelm, 21, 155n15
Dionysus, 133
Don Quixote, 57, 161n7; *see also* Cervantes Saavedra, Miguel de
Dostoevsky, Feodor Mikhailovich, 98
Dumas, Alexandre, 19
Dusany, Edward John Moreton Drax Plunkett, Baron, 28

Editorial Azar, 34
Education, 41–44, 71, 79–80, 108–11

Education, Ministry of, 35
Einstein, Albert, 84–85, 159n8
England, 40, 41, 67, 75, 151
Escorial, El, 18, 57
Escorial, University of El, 29
Escuela de Institutrices, 16
Escuela Superior del Magisterio, 22, 23
España, 24, 46, 62, 152
Espasa Calpe, 26, 32
Espectador, El, 24–25, 26, 28, 51, 62, 76, 77
Estoril, 34
Europa, 23, 152
Europäische Revue, 32
Existentialism, 116, 117

Falange Española, 32
Faro, 22, 23, 152
Fascism, 88, 108, 113
Ferdinand of Aragón, 73
Florence, 23
Forster, Edward Morgan, 159n9
France, 30, 33, 46, 67, 75, 86, 151
Francis of Assisi, Saint, 49
Franco, Francisco, 34
Franks, 75
Freud, Sigmund, 99–100, 159n10
Frobenius, Leo, 94

Galileo, 121
Ganivet, Angel, 63
Gaos, José, 127
García, Félix, 35
Gasset Chinchilla, María de los Dolores, 18
Gasset Chinchilla, Rafael, 18
Gasset y Artime, Eduardo, 17, 18
Generation of 1898, 17, 22, 24, 37, 38, 50, 152
Generation of 1914, 37
Generation of 1927, 27
Geneva, 35
Germany, 32, 41, 43, 53, 67, 86, 151; and the visits of Ortega, 21, 22, 23, 35, 37, 39, 40, 61, 148
Giner de los Ríos, Francisco, 16, 17, 155nl, 157n9
Giotto, 130
Glasgow, University of, 35

God, 57, 82, 83, 92, 105, 121
Goethe, Johann Wolfgang von, 35, 83, 119, 121, 132, 133
Gothic culture, 48
Goya, Francisco José de, 121, 129, 132–33, 158n15
Gracián, Baltasar, 129
Granada, 18
Granada, University of, 32
Granja, La, 34, 35
Greece, 59, 128, 133, 142
Grenoble, 33
Guadalajara, 18

Hague, The, 33
Hamburg, 35
Harvard University, 33
Heidegger, Martin, 35, 103, 156n33; *Sein und Zeit*, 103–104
Hero, 60–61
Historical reason, 95, 116, 125–26, 127, 129, 133, 140, 146
Historiography, 119–22, 159n5
History, philosophy of, 78, 83, 93–95, 106, 110, 116, 125, 138–43, 148
Hitler, Adolf, 87
Hoffmann, Heinrich, 53, 54
Holland, 32, 33
Hugo, Victor, 46
Huizinga, Johann, 33, 34; *Homo Ludens*, 34
Husserl, Edmund, 53, 54, 57, 76; *Ideen zu einer reinen Phänomenologie*, 53

Idealism, 39, 47, 53, 61, 92–93, 96, 105–106, 118
Imparcial, El, 17, 18, 20, 23, 25, 69
Impressionism, 49, 52, 58, 95
Institución Libre de Enseñanza, 16, 17, 19, 23, 43
Instituto de Humanidades, 34, 35
Irrationalism, 59
Isabel II, 15, 17
Isabella of Castile, 73
Italy, 86

Jaén, 31
James, William, 57
Jesuits, *see* Jesus, Society of

Jesus, Society of, 19, 36
Jiménez, Juan Ramón, 156n17
Julius Caesar, 159n2
Juntas de Defensa, 25, 69–71

Kant, Immanuel, 16, 21, 25; *Critique of Pure Reason*, 21; *see also* Neo-Kantianism
Krause, Karl Christian Friedrich, 16
Krausism, 16, 17, 43

Language, 146–47, 162n17
League of Nations, 62, 68
Leibniz, Gottfried Wilhelm, 34, 92, 96, 137, 138, 162n10
Leiden, 33
Leipzig, 20, 21
León, 31
Liberalism, 39–41, 45, 65, 69, 71, 138–39
Liberal Party, 45, 66, 88
Liga de Educación Política, 23–24, 44–46, 112
Lisbon, 29, 133, 134
Lisbon, University of, 34
Logos, 127
London, 35
Lorraine, Claude, 129
Lunes, Los, 17, 18
Lutoslawski, W., 155n2
Luz, 31

Machado, Antonio, 30, 33, 153
Madrid, 22, 23, 24, 33, 34, 35, 46, 71, 90, 91, 131, 132, 133
Madrid, University of, 20, 23, 29, 32, 34
Maeztu, Ramiro de, 20, 22, 38, 87
Marañón, Gregorio, 30, 33, 112, 160n12
Marburg, 21, 23, 35, 42, 43, 47, 53, 56, 135
Marías, Julián, 34, 56, 58
Marrero, Domingo, 20
Marseilles, 33
Martínez, Manuel, 18
Martínez Ruiz, José, 55, 157n1
Marx, Karl, 69
Marxism, 22, 41
Maura, Antonio, 28
Maura, Gabriel, 22

Maura, Miguel, 31
Mediterranean culture, 48, 49, 58
Mencken, Henry Louis, 160n19
Mendoza, 25
Menéndez Pelayo, Marcelino, 37, 38
Menéndez Pidal, Ramón, 33
Mesopotamia, 142
Metaphor, 47, 54–55, 97, 134, 158n17
Mirabeau, Honoré Gabriel Riquetti,
   comte de, 28, 89, 90, 91, 121, 132
Miraflores del Palo, 19
Monarchy, 45, 67, 70, 73, 89, 90, 112–
   14, 141
Montevideo, 29
Moors, 73, 75
Morocco, 69
Morón Arroyo, Ciriaco, 61, 158n4,
   159n7, 159n11, 161n8
Munich, 35
Munich, University of, 35
Mussolini, Benito, 87, 108
Mysticism, 38, 84, 102

Nación, La, 29, 138
Natorp, Paul, 21, 39, 43
Navarro Ledesma, Francisco, 155n8,
   155n13
Neo-Kantianism, 21, 39, 43, 53, 61, 135
Nietzsche, Friedrich, 17, 20, 21, 43, 83
Nihilism, 52
Nostrand, Howard Lee, 116
Nouvelle Revue Française, 26
Novel, 51–53, 59–61, 97–99

Ocampo, Victoria, 33
Oestgeest, 33
Ortega Munilla, José, 17–18, 19, 21, 25,
   26
Ortega Spottorno, Miguel Germán, 23
Ortega Spottorno, Soledad, 33
Ortega y Gasset, Eduardo, 18, 19, 27,
   33, 35, 87, 159n1
Ortega y Gasset, José, youth, 18–19;
   university education, 19–21; in Ger-
   many, 20–21; early publications,
   22–24; and El Sol, 25–30; and
   Dictatorship, 27–30; second trip to
   South America, 29; and the Republic,
   30–32; in exile, 32–34; in South
   America, 33–34; the last years, 34–36

WORKS:
"Adán en el Paraíso," 47
"El amor en Stendhal," 101–103
"Apuntes sobre el pensamiento. Su
   teurgia y demiurgia," 127–28
"Arte de este mundo y del otro,"
   48–49
Las Atlántidas, 93–95, 107
"Bajo el arco en ruina," 25, 69
"El caso Italia," 23
"Conciencia, objeto y las tres distan-
   cias de éste," 76–77
"Conversación en el 'golf' o la idea del
   'dharma'," 28
"De Europa meditatio quaedam," 35
Del Imperio Romano, 138–39
"Del optimismo en Leibniz," 34
La deshumanización del arte, 28,
   96–97
"Ensayo de estética a manera de pró-
   logo," 53, 54–55
En torno a Galileo, 119–22
"Epílogo sobre el alma de-
   silusionada," 84
España invertebrada, 26, 62, 72–76,
   86, 106
El espíritu de la letra, 28
Estudios sobre el amor, 28, 101–103
"El genio de la guerra y la guerra
   alemana," 67
Goya, 132–33
"Hegel y la historiología," 29
"Historia como sistema," 124–25, 126
El hombre y la gente, 143–47
"Ideal del teatro," 34, 133–34
La idea de principio en Leibniz y la
   evolución de la teoría deductiva,
   134–38
"Ideas políticas," 28, 90–91
Ideas sobre la novela, 28, 97–99
"Ideas sobre Pío Baroja," 51–53
"Ideas y creencias," 125–26
Una interpretación de las historia
   universal, 139–43
"Introducción al presente," 29
"Introducción a Velázquez," 34
Unas lecciones de metafísica, 116–18
"Máscaras," 133–34
"Más sobre el caso Italia," 23
Meditación de Europe, 147–49

"Meditacíon de la técnica," 122
Meditaciones del Quijote, 24, 55–61, 62, 77, 98, 104, 105
"Mirabeau," 88–89
La misión de la universidad, 108–11
"La misión del bibliotecario," 124
"Nada 'moderno' y 'muy siglo XX'," 77–78
"Ni vitalismo ni racionalismo," 92
"El ocaso de las revoluciones," 83–84
"Origen y epílogo de la filosofía," 128–29
"La pedagogía social como programa social," 43
Personas, obras y cosas, 150
"Pidiendo un Goethe desde dentro," 118–19
"Pío Baroja: anatomía de un alma dispersa," 51–52
"Una primera vista sobre Baroja," 51–52
¿Qué es filosofía?, 29, 103–106
"¿Qué es la técnica?," 32
"El *Quijote* en la escuela," 79
La rebelión de las masas, 106–108, 109
"Rectificación de la República," 31, 116
La redención de las provincias, 90–91
"Sensación, construcción e intuición," 53
"El sentido histórico de la teoría de Einstein," 84–85
"Sobre el concepto de sensación," 53–54
"Sobre el facismo," 28
"Sobre el punto de vista en las artes," 95–96
El tema de nuestro tiempo, 26, 62, 80–83, 92
"Los terrores del año mil," 20
"Verdad y perspectiva," 77–78
"Vieja y nueva política," 24, 32, 44, 65
"Vitalidad, alma, espíritu," 100–101
"¡Viva la República!," 116

Ortega y Gasset, Rafaela, 33

Panza, Sancho, 60
Papelera Española, La, 25
Paradise, 48, 157n12

Paris, 20, 26, 32, 33, 68
Parliament, 66, 70, 72, 73, 86, 90–91, 113
Parmenides, 136
Particularism, 72–75, 86
Pérez de Ayala, Ramón, 30, 33, 112, 160n2
Pérez Galdós, Benito, "Episodios Nacionales," 19
Perspectivism, 48, 57, 77–78, 83, 84–85, 93–94
Phenomenology, 53–54, 61
Philip II, 18
Philip III, 73
Philip IV, 130
Philosophy, 53, 104–106, 110, 122, 128–29, 135–38
Plato, 49, 56, 92, 102, 135
Portugal, 33, 34
Positivism, 77, 96, 105
Poussin, Nicolas, 129
Primo de Rivera, José Antonio, 32, 156n31
Primo de Rivera, Miguel, 27, 29, 30, 86–87, 112
Proust, Marcel, 99
Psychology, 53, 60, 99–101
Puerto Rico, University of, 35

Quixote, Don, *see* Don Quixote
Quixotism, 57

Raphael, 95
Rationalism, 59, 77, 81–84, 92–93
Ratiovitalism, 81, 95, 100, 116, 118–19
Real Sociedad Vascongada de Amigos del País, 34
Realism, 118
Relationships, 47–48, 56–57, 58
Relativism, 81, 83
Renan, Ernest, 46–47
Recontres Internationales, 35
Republicanism, 45
Republic of 1931, 24, 28, 37, 90, 112–16
Republican Reform Party, 23
Residencia de Estudiantes, 26, 33
Revista de Occidente, 24, 26–28, 34, 86, 87, 99, 152; Ortega's work published in, 92, 95
Ribera, José, 129

Ríos, Fernando de los, 19, 29
Río y Labandeira, José del, 19
Roman Empire, 134, 138–42
Romanticism, 46, 97, 121, 132
Rome, 75, 138–42
Rosario, 25
Rotterdam, 33
"Rubín de Cendoya," 155n5

Sagasta, Práxedes, 15
Saint-Jean-de-Luz, 18, 33
Salamanca, University of, 20
Salmerón, Nicolás, 23
Sanjurjo, José, 32
San Sebastián, 34
Santander, 32
Santiago de Chile, 29
Sanz del Río, Julián, 16, 20
Schapp, Wilhelm, 158n20
Scheler, Max, 56, 67–68, 159n11; Der
    Genius des Kriegs und der deutsche
    Krieg, 67
Scholasticism, 135, 137
Schwarz, Egon, 161n12
Science, and culture, 46, 48, 58, 107,
    126; and education, 79, 109–11; and
    philosophy, 93, 94, 104–105, 121, 125,
    135–38; as discipline, 39, 41, 42–43,
    97
Segovia, 30, 34
Seville, 32, 130
Simmel, Georg, 21
Socialism, 22, 39–41, 44, 45, 69, 71,
    157n8
Socialist Party, 23, 40, 88
Socialist Republican Party, 113
Sociedad de Amigos del Arte, 29
Socrates, 81, 82
Sol, El, 25, 26, 27, 28, 29, 30, 32, 62, 86;
    Ortega's work published in, 72, 88,
    90, 96, 97, 101, 106
Sorel, Georges, 69
Spengler, Oswald, 72, 94, 139; The De-
    cline of the West, 72
Sport, 80, 83, 93, 97, 134
Spottorno y Topete, Rosa, 23, 33
Starling, Ernest Henry, 79
Stendhal, see Beyle, Marie Henri
Stoics, 135, 137
Stuttgart, 32

Syndicalism, 45, 108

Taine, Hippolyte, 46
Technology, 42, 45, 79, 122, 161n15
Torquay, 35
Toynbee, Arnold, 139–40, 142, 148, 149,
    162n12; A Study of History, 139
Tripoli, 23
Tronche, La, 33
Tucumán, 25
Tutankhamun, 159n4

Uexküll, Jakob Johann von, 57
Unamuno, Miguel de, as guide of
    Ortega, 37, 38, 39, 103, 157n3; Del
    sentimiento trágico de la vida, 24, 59;
    politics of, 23, 31, 87, 114; relations
    with Ortega, 20, 22, 27, 32, 36, 50,
    150, 151, 157n5
United Nations, 140
Universidad Internacional Menéndez
    Pelayo, 32
Urgoiti, Nicolás María de, 25, 26, 30
Uruguay, 35
Utilitarianism, 77, 78, 80
Utopianism, 82, 84, 85

Valladolid, 35
Van Dyck, Anthony, 129
Velázquez, Diego de, 95, 129–32
Venezuela, 35
Venice, 35
Verne, Jules, 19
Vichy, 33
Viète, François, 137
Visigoths, 75
Vitalism, 76–80, 99, 103
Vital reason, see Ratiovitalism
Vives, Juan, 121

Weimar, 119, 132
Woman, 102–103, 159n12, 160n14
World War I, 37, 62, 66, 67, 68, 69, 72,
    77
Wundt, Wilhelm, 20
Württemburg, 35

Zaragoza, 22, 132
Zumaya, 34
Zurbarán, Francisco de, 129